RELIGIOUS FREEDOM IN A CHANGING WORLD

RELIGIOUS FREEDOM IN A CHANGING WORLD

Ninan Koshy

BOOK SERIES

WCC Publications, Geneva

BV
741
.K67
1992

Cover design: Rob Lucas

ISBN 2-8254-1047-0

© 1992 WCC Publications, World Council of Churches,
150 route de Ferney, P.O. Box 2100, 1211 Geneva 2, Switzerland

Risk Book Series No. 54

Printed in Switzerland

*To the memory
of my mother Mariam*

Contents

FOREWORD ix

1. INTRODUCTION 1
2. THE SITUATION TODAY 6
3. UNDERSTANDING RELIGIOUS LIBERTY 22
4. RELIGIOUS LIBERTY AND THE STATE 33
5. RELIGIONS AND RELIGIOUS LIBERTY 50
6. SOME NEW DEVELOPMENTS 57
7. THE WCC AND RELIGIOUS LIBERTY 73
8. THE ROMAN CATHOLIC CHURCH AND RELIGIOUS LIBERTY 86
9. THE UNITED NATIONS AND RELIGIOUS LIBERTY . . 96
10. CONCLUSION 111

Foreword

A continual reflection on religious liberty is not only of theoretical interest but a necessity in these days of intense and frequent encounters of people with different faiths and convictions. It has been suggested by some legal scholars that religious liberty had no distinct character of its own and that its components could be subsumed by other rights and liberties, in particular the rights to freedom of expression and freedom of association. Such an approach not only misinterprets the essence of religious liberty as an individual right, but also underestimates the vital function of religious liberty for peacefully living together in multi-religious societies. Quite appropriately, the promotion and protection of religious liberty is now moving up on the international human rights agenda.

Since the second world war, strenuous efforts have been made, at the level of the United Nations and in other international forums, to strengthen the normative basis of religious liberty. These efforts have not only focused on the substantive scope of religious freedom but also sought to tackle theories and practices of discrimination based on religion or belief. The aspect of freedom and the aspect of non-discrimination are — as should never be overlooked — integral and indivisible parts of religious liberty.

From the outset the World Council of Churches, through its Commission of the Churches on International Affairs (CCIA), has been closely involved in these efforts of setting effective and just standards on freedom and non-discrimination in matters of religion or belief. At the same time the ecumenical movement was mindful that standard-setting without developing and applying a corresponding praxis would lack sufficient credibility. Therefore, it asserted that any effective involvement in the issue of religious liberty must begin with critical self-examination and also that religious liberty should never be used as a pretext to claim privileges which are not due to all sectors of society. It may be added that such an approach is also a precondition for any meaningful dialogue with people of different faiths and convictions.

The book now before us reflects that same approach. It is the fruit of an in-depth analysis of the nature and the implications of religious liberty. The author, Ninan Koshy, has a long record of dedicated service in the ecumenical movement, notably as a former director of the Commission of the Churches on International Affairs (CCIA). In that position he has gained deep insights into the role of religion in national and international society, and he has also had to deal, from the perspective of the churches, with the roots and extent of religious conflict affecting the life and well-being of many people.

As a person who has had the privilege of being closely associated with Ninan Koshy's work for many years, I am particularly pleased and gratified that he is now sharing his knowledge and insights on the question of religious liberty with a broader constituency. I am confident that this book will enable interested readers to arrive at a deeper understanding of the various issues analyzed in this study.

THEO VAN BOVEN
Former moderator
Commission of the Churches
on International Affairs, WCC

1. Introduction

Religious liberty, a perennial question, has emerged as a prominent issue in the contemporary world. Not a day passes without some reference in the media to religious freedom somewhere around the globe. Whether it is the decree against Salman Rushdie or the imprisonment of a prominent Egyptian novelist, the issue of religious freedom is raised. It comes up when discussing educational systems, school prayers and school dress codes. The founder of a New Religious Movement is imprisoned for violating fiscal laws in the United States, and claims are made that his religious liberty is under attack. One state enacts a law against conversion — and calls it the Freedom of Religions Act. Another introduces a law which would make sermons which the government considers "political" punishable — and gives it the name Religious Harmony Act.

The World Council of Churches made a declaration on religious liberty at its first assembly in Amsterdam (1948). It was an issue that the Council had already addressed during the period of its formation; and the Amsterdam declaration not only laid down the fundamental principles of religious liberty but underlined its international significance.

To be sure, the Amsterdam declaration was conditioned by the times. The world had just come out of the trauma of the second world war. The founding of the United Nations had given new hope for a peaceful world. But next to these great expectations were new fears and uncertainties. The cold war had already started. The vast majority of churches from Eastern Europe were not represented at Amsterdam. Seen from a predominantly Western perspective influenced by missionary experiences, events in many other parts of the world were also disturbing. There were revolutionary movements and independence struggles, and it was unclear how they would affect liberties in general, religious liberty in particular and the fellowship of the churches.

The Council addressed the issue of religious liberty often in the succeeding years. The evolution in the ecumenical understanding of religious liberty reflected the new experiences of the churches. As the constituency of the Council expanded, new problems in religious liberty were encountered and new perspectives were added. The mission of the church in each place brought new insights to the worldwide church.

Fundamental principles of religious liberty are of universal application. While these principles are non-negotiable, the Council recognized that in practice there were limits to religious freedom in most situations. Religious liberty in full measure was achieved nowhere.

The situation of each member church was conditioned by a variety of factors. History, tradition, church-state relations, theological understanding, privileges, intercommunity relations, foreign policy and the international political climate all played a part in deciding the extent and scope of religious liberty in each situation. Political upheavals invariably brought in new models of church-state relations and a new situation of religious liberty. Many churches equated loss of traditional privileges with loss of religious freedom, and the distinction between the two was not always clear.

While it is always important to uphold the fundamental principles of religious liberty everywhere, it is useful to look at each situation in pragmatic terms and see whether there is more religious freedom, or less religious freedom, whether the zone of liberty is expanding or contracting. When there is a change for the worse in a country the fellowship of churches elsewhere in the world should try to see how best to support the affected churches.

This has been the general approach of the World Council of Churches. It is true that in some instances, even when the WCC knew of persecution of the church in particular and religion in general, it has been hesitant to denounce the government. Rather, it has carefully monitored such situations, exploring means by which the freedom of the church there could be regained or expanded while ensuring that it is able to continue in the fellowship of the Council. This policy has been part of a general WCC policy on human rights, in which the models of action range from public denunciation to behind-the-scenes diplomacy.

The Russian Orthodox Church, which is the largest member church of the Council, joined the fellowship only in 1961. This period was one of severe persecution of the church in the Soviet Union. The leaders of the WCC were fully aware of the limitations of the situation and their consequences. Yet the freedom to be part of the ecumenical fellowship was a valuable one for the Russian Orthodox Church, and its coming into the WCC was an enrichment of the worldwide church. The history of the WCC's relations with the Russian Orthodox Church provides a fascinating case study of the impact of religious liberty in a country on the global fellowship of churches.

The situation of the churches in the former Soviet Union and elsewhere in Eastern and Central Europe at the beginning of the 1990s is vastly different from what it was when they joined the WCC. But the dramatic changes of the late 1980s in these countries should not make us oblivious to the gradual expansion of religious liberty there over the years and to the role played by churches in some of those countries in preparing the stage for the drama, using the freedom they had as churches.

Other significant experiences have influenced the WCC's understanding of and policies on religious liberty. Four churches from China were members of the Council at the time of the Amsterdam assembly. But the position the WCC took on the Korean war two years later led to the resignation of one of its presidents, T.C. Chao from China, and the de facto withdrawal of the Chinese churches. That was part of the story. The other part is that soon after Amsterdam, communists came to power in China and a new policy on religion came into force. A number of WCC statements in the 1950s reflected concern about religious freedom in China, though often indirectly.

A major change in the religious policy of the People's Republic of China in the late 1970s enabled the church there to renew its relations with churches outside; and the church in China rejoined the membership of the World Council of Churches at the seventh assembly in Canberra in 1991.

Also present in Canberra were representatives of the small Christian community in the Democratic People's Republic of Korea. Isolated for more than four decades, the church in North Korea was brought into the fellowship of the worldwide church, in spite of severe limitations in the situation, by the WCC's engagement in the issues of justice and peace in the region. Until four years ago, North Korean authorities did not acknowledge that there was a church in the country. Today, for the first time in forty years, there are church buildings in Pyongyang, attesting to the Christian presence there.

The experiences of the churches in what is generally known as the third world were of considerable significance for WCC thinking on religious liberty. Despite differences from country to country, there were also some common features. At the time of the Amsterdam assembly very few were members of the Council. By the 1960s they had become an important component, whose influence grew rapidly. It was natural that the WCC's attention turned to the struggles for human dignity and justice in these countries.

As ecumenical solidarity with such struggles was strengthened, religious liberty came to be seen as more and more integrated with other human rights. The emergence of Marxist-oriented governments in some third-world countries in the 1970s created new problems for the churches. Their policies on religion were often influenced by experiences in Eastern Europe. But there was a new dimension to the issue of religious liberty in some of them where the struggle for independence and liberation was supported by at least a section of the churches and the World Council of Churches.

The 1970s also brought new challenges in pluralism. Two developments took place. Religious revival, especially in Islam, led to implementation or strengthening of religious-based laws in some countries. Minority communities experienced a high degree of intolerance even in countries traditionally noted for their great tolerance. At the same time, religions other than Christianity were growing in a number of Western countries. Both developments created new experiences for churches and raised new questions about religious liberty.

The variety of experiences of churches within the WCC means that the Council must regularly monitor the situation of religious liberty in all parts of the world and consider carefully the basic issues involved. Such consideration has been influenced by the ongoing struggles for, and the evolution in thinking on, human rights.

In 1963, the World Council of Churches published *The Basis of Religious Liberty*,[1] by A.F. Carillo de Albornoz. It grew out of a study by the Council's Secretariat for Religious Liberty to find "a solidly established basis for our Christian attitude concerning religious freedom". The outstanding theological and legal scholarship reflected in this major contribution to the international discussion on religious liberty makes this study highly significant even today.

* * *

The present book is necessarily limited in its scope. Its main purpose is to place the evolution of ecumenical thinking on religious liberty in the context of new developments around the world and in the international community. Because this is a rather ambitious undertaking in view of the complexity and breadth of the subject, deliberate limits have been imposed on the topics dealt with. Some issues are only just touched on — including the complex issue of religion and politics.

We begin by examining the nature of religious liberty and the links between religious freedom and other human rights. The critical role played by the state in deciding the extent of religious liberty is considered. After briefly looking at the role of the church vis-a-vis religious liberty, we analyze some of the new and significant developments.

The evolution of ecumenical thinking on religious liberty is traced through the statements of the WCC. This methodology has two limitations: the policies of the WCC on religious liberty in specific situations are not mentioned, and the remarkable contribution by confessional families to ecumenical thinking on religious liberty is omitted.

The position of the Roman Catholic Church is examined in some detail. This has long been a matter of concern to the WCC, for the Roman Catholic position has influenced the policies of many states, as well as the freedom of other churches.

Intergovernmental and international instruments today play a more important role in dealing with religious liberty than ever before. Our chapter on this, however, has to be limited to the United Nations system. That system also provides a useful entry point into our discussion. To sketch a picture of religious liberty in the world today we have drawn on reports of the Special Rapporteur of the UN Human Rights Commission on the Declaration on the Elimination of All Forms of Intolerance and of Discrimination Based on Religion or Belief.

NOTE

[1] A.F. Carillo de Albornoz, *The Basis of Religious Liberty*, London, SCM, 1963.

2. The Situation Today

For several years the United Nations Commission on Human Rights has engaged a Special Rapporteur to monitor compliance with the UN Declaration on the Elimination of All Forms of Intolerance and of Discrimination Based on Religion or Belief. A survey of his report on alleged violations of the provisions of this Declaration and on the responses made by the governments concerned provides a useful starting point for our discussion.[1] The cases cited in this chapter not only illustrate some of the ways in which religious liberty is being violated today, but also suggest how various governments understand religious freedom and their obligation to ensure it.

Because the work of the Special Rapporteur focuses on instances brought to his attention through the particular mechanisms of the UN system, the following examples should be seen as illustrative rather than offering a country-by-country "report card" on the global situation of religious liberty. (We shall discuss religious freedom within the context of the UN in greater detail in chapter 9.) In what follows, the order of examples considered, taken from the report of 1991, is alphabetical by country.

The Special Rapporteur wrote to Albania's government on 5 October 1990 that

> there has been no news of the Jesuit priest, Father Ndoc Luli, of Mali Jushit, who was allegedly imprisoned in 1980 after having baptized the child of a member of his family. In addition, a 45 year-old Albanian citizen of Greek ethnic origin, Klearchos Papasavos, of Drim Himara Viona, is allegedly serving a long prison sentence on account of his religious beliefs.

The government replied on 12 December that Papasavos was "free and able to exercise all his rights, like all other Albanian citizens". As to Fr Ndoc Luli, "the appropriate authorities have carried out the necessary checks and there is no mention of his name in the relevant records; in other words he is unknown".

On 8 November 1989 the Bulgarian government was advised of the allegation "that Baptists have not been able to hold a congress since 1946 and that the government, rather than the Baptists themselves, has been appointing the leaders of their churches. Thus, the Baptists are allegedly being denied their right to meet freely and to elect their own leaders."

In its reply of 11 January 1990, the government said that "the acting chairman of the Baptist Church Union in the People's Republic of Bulgaria, Mr Yordan Gospodinov, has confirmed the forthcoming convening of the Baptist church congress in this country to elect new Union leaders". The Baptists themselves agreed, according to the government, that the delay in holding a congress was due to "internal contradictions among various leadership bodies and personalities of the Baptist church".

Another communication was sent to the Bulgarian government on 24 September 1990:

> According to information received, Bulgarian Muslims of Turkish ethnic origin in the town of Kurdzhali, who allegedly resisted a forced assimilation campaign initiated in December 1984, had their houses and property taken away from them before being sent to prison or exiled inside Bulgaria. According to other information, material used in the Bulgarian educational curriculum contains a large number of expressions that encourage discrimination against Muslim Bulgarians of Turkish origin.

The government's reply spoke of changes in policy after November 1989 and after free democratic elections in June 1990. The council of state and council of ministers of Bulgaria had condemned all actions infringing on the right to a free choice of name and religious belief and had affirmed the right of every citizen to speak languages other than Bulgarian in everyday life and to adhere to his or her customs. Moreover, the law to amend and supplement the constitution proclaimed the freedom of religious propaganda, and the Bulgarian Citizens' Names Law made it possible to restore forcibly changed names, under an accelerated court procedure and later under administrative procedure.

According to information received by the Special Rapporteur and passed to the government of Burundi, "at a meeting of governors of provinces in February 1989 attended by the president of the republic, it was recommended that the parochial activities of Jehovah's Witnesses in Burundi should be limited and that Jehovah's Witnesses who were arrested should be severely punished". The communication went on to give instances of arrests and beating of Jehovah's Witnesses and the incitement by a provincial governor to attack them.

Burundi is "engaged in struggles on several fronts, among which that for national unity is not the least important", the government replied, noting that it reserved the right to grant or refuse authorization to religious sects, though a refusal "has to be justified, for instance by consideration of public order, if, for example, a sect's objectives run counter to the ideals of peace, justice and the unity of the people of Burundi".

The government said the Jehovah's Witnesses have "recently been importuning the entire international community" with their allegation of persecution. Not only did they engage in activities in Burundi — illegally, since they were not authorized — but they were instilling "ideas and practices which are contrary to the traditional values of the people of Burundi". Claiming to eschew politics, they were inciting people "not to salute the national flag, not to respect authority and to cease work on the day of prayer, all of which is contrary to the essential values of the people of Burundi, and encourages them to disregard their civic duties".

A communication to the government of the People's Republic of China on 8 November 1989 mentioned reports that the authorities had announced that "no further admission of monks in the monasteries of Tibet will be tolerated and no monasteries may be renovated without the government's approval" and that two of the largest monasteries were surrounded by armed troops. It also referred to allegations that monks and nuns had been arrested, detained and killed in connection with a peaceful demonstration in Lhasa on 5 March 1989, and that six nuns had been sentenced to three years' hard labour and re-education for chanting slogans calling for Tibetan independence.

The Chinese government replied that the incident in Lhasa, which they called "a riot staged through violence and terrorist means" and "by no means a 'peaceful demonstration'", "was aimed at splitting Chinese territory and undermining unity among nationalities". The measures taken to stop the riot according to law "had nothing to do with the affairs of the temples or the normal activities of the people practising religion".

The government said the arrests were made because the monks and nuns took part in activities of splitting China. The six nuns received a three-year rehabilitation-through-labour sentence because theirs was a minor offence of instigating activities for the "independence of Tibet" during a folk custom festival in Lhasa.

A second communication to China on 15 June 1990 spoke of accounts of the arrest of several Roman Catholic priests in northern China, reportedly in connection with the implementation of new policy directives issued by the authorities in February 1989, according to which Catholics who remain loyal to the Vatican and carry out religious activities outside the government-recognized church should be "severely dealt with in accordance with the law".

The Chinese government insisted that the charge

> that priests were put into prison without trial does not tally with facts. None except Fan Xueyan is a Catholic bishop. The examination and punishment of these people have nothing to do with religious belief... Fan Xueyan was a former Catholic bishop of the Baoding diocese. He was sentenced to fixed-term imprisonment of ten years in 1983 for he collaborated with foreign religious forces in interfering with the religious affairs of China, which endangered the national sovereignty.

On 5 October 1990, the Special Rapporteur wrote once again to the Chinese government about the situation in Tibet, where, it said, many monks and nuns had been expelled from monasteries and nunneries in the Lhasa area or are in detention without any specific charges brought against them...

> Once in their regions, the monks and nuns are relegated to performing agricultural work, their movements are restricted and controlled and they are forbidden to leave their home towns. In addition, they are not allowed to shave their heads, join any other religious institutions, practise religion in public or perform religious services for households.

The reply from the Chinese government said:

> A few Tibetan monks and nuns, incited by separatists abroad, repeatedly participated in the activities of splitting the country and stirring up riots since the fall of 1987. These activities violated the Chinese constitution and relevant laws and seriously disrupted the national security and social order... Some of these monks and nuns have been punished by judicial organs for their crimes, others have

returned to their ancestral homes... It must be pointed out that respect for and protection of the freedom of religious belief is a consistent stand and a basic policy of the Chinese government. No one who violates the law can escape from due punishment. The fact that some criminal monks and nuns have been punished according to the law has nothing to do with religious belief.

A communication from the Special Rapporteur to the government of Colombia on 5 October 1990 mentioned information received about death threats made against members of religious communities by paramilitary groups who accused them of engaging in subversive activities. Some of them, it was said, had been assassinated. The sources claimed that the persons in question were the victims of violence because of their community and church work.

In its reply, the Colombian government gave details about its investigations of the cases which, it said, "fall within the context of the complex violence, attributable to many causes, that has affected Colombia, although, in the opinion of the government, they cannot be attributed to state action or to state coercion against freedom of conscience in a country where the majority are overwhelmingly Catholic".

No reply had been received by March 1991 to a September 1990 letter to the government of the Dominican Republic conveying information according to which "some members of the Maranatajoraalingin Church, of Swedish origin, established in the Dominican Republic, allegedly suffered a number of human rights violations, apparently because they belong to this religion".

In a communication of 15 June 1990 to the government of Egypt, the Special Rapporteur enquired about "acts of discrimination against Egyptian citizens of the Christian faith, affecting also their property, churches and associations [which] have occurred in Upper Egypt, particularly in Menya, Abu Qierqas, Eeni Mazar and the villages of Beni Ebid and Al-Berba".

The government of Egypt replied on 4 October that

> the discovery of immoral and illicit relations between members of the Muslim and Christian communities gave rise to a form of intercommunal tension, which escalated in the light of the customs and traditions prevailing in the southern part of the country (Upper

Egypt)... The Egyptian constitution stipulates that all Egyptian citizens are equal before the law, without distinction on grounds of sex, origin, language or religion. The constitution also guarantees freedom of belief and freedom of religious observance. The causes of most intercommunal tension can be found in everyday occurrence (quarrels, disputes) to which some parties endeavour to attach confessional significance.

In response to later enquiries about reports of two instances in which Egyptian Muslims who had converted to Christianity and six Egyptian Christians, including a priest and his wife, were murdered, the government wrote that "the state authorities take all the requisite measures, in accordance with the law, in the event of any behaviour likely to prejudice national unity. This was done following the above-mentioned incidents."

In a communication of 6 November 1990 to the government of El Salvador, the Special Rapporteur referred to many complaints about "disturbing violations of the human rights of religious leaders or of the helpers of the country's churches" since a state of siege was declared there a year earlier. Large numbers of persons were said to be persecuted "for belonging to specific religious denominations which are involved, out of social commitment, in work with the underprivileged classes of society. Although these cases have taken place in a situation of widespread violence, the sources indicate that the persons have allegedly been the victims of violence on account of their community and church work." Among the instances cited was the assassination of six Jesuit priests, their housekeeper and her daughter at the Central American University of San Salvador. The Special Rapporteur pointed out that all nine members of the St John the Baptist Episcopal Church arrested by the National Guard were members of the Association for the Development of Awareness for Man's Spiritual and Economic Revival (CREDITO), a social programme of the Episcopal Church. Furthermore, he said, foreign helpers of churches were being detained and expelled and local church leaders were the target of harassment and death threats. At the time the report was released in March no reply had come from the government.

Nor was a response received to a letter to the government of Ghana asking about an alleged freeze imposed on any activity by Jehovah's Witnesses.

The Special Rapporteur asked the government of Greece about reports that the Greek Muslim minority of Turkish origin in Western Thrace were prevented from entering the main mosque and that Jehovah's Witnesses were imprisoned for refusing conscription.

The government replied that access to the mosque was obstructed since police had to intervene in clashes between "extremist elements of the aforesaid minority" and some Christian elements. It added that "Jehovah's Witnesses in Greece are free to exercise their belief. As a matter of fact, the Greek constitution provides for freedom of religious conscience and worship." However, because "Jehovah's Witness faith is not recognized in Greece as a religion..., its self-proclaimed 'priests' are not exempted from military service".

In a communication to the government of India, the Special Rapporteur wrote that "it has been reported that since November 1989 members of the Ananda Marga community and their sympathizers in Purulia District, West Bengal, have constantly been harassed or intimidated".

The government replied that "far from there being any harassment or intimidation of the Ananda Marga community and their sympathizers, the latter have, in fact, been indulging in various acts of violence in different parts of the state of West Bengal", adding that "the Ananda Marg, under the garb of religion, has been known not only for its violence and terrorism, but also for its sinister chauvinism, which is evident in its activities through its frontal organizations, like Amra Bengali".

The Special Rapporteur informed the Indonesian government of allegations that a number of followers of the Jehovah's Witness faith, the Association of San Antonio and the so-called Usroh groups "have been arrested and sentenced to prison terms for practising their faith".

After stating that "the Republic of Indonesia is a democratic state which promotes and protects the rights of all its citizens to practise the religion of their choice", the government said that while it does not "interfere in the internal matters of each religion, this does not imply that it would remain indifferent should there be activities which could disrupt the three principles for religious harmony: the internal matters of each religion, the relation between and among adherents and the relation between adherents and the government". The "Jehovah Witness sect", it said, was banned in Indonesia by a government decree of 7 December 1976 "since its teaching and practices are contrary to the true Christian faith". Regarding the Association of San Antonio, the government replied that "shortly after its inception (in 1963) it was banned by the Roman Catholic Church because its beliefs stood in direct contradiction to those taught and adhered to by the church".

A communication to the government of the Islamic Republic of Iran took up several cases:

> It has been alleged that the Iranian Bible Society, based in Teheran, which operated legally and openly for ten years, had been closed at the beginning of 1990...
>
> It is alleged that as of 1980-81, religious education was abolished in most Armenian schools. It is also alleged that all Christian Armenian principals of schools were removed by a governmental decree and replaced by principals who were proven faithful Muslims. Starting with the academic year 1983-84, religious education was reportedly prohibited in all Armenian schools without exception... Starting with the academic year 1985-86, it is alleged that parents were forced to sign papers promising not to allow their daughters to attend schools without an Islamic veil, despite the fact that Armenian girls of Christian faith attended schools wearing scarves covering their hair and neck...
>
> It has been reported that despite certain individual improvements in their situation, members of the Baha'i community continue to be subjected to intolerance based on religion and belief. It is alleged that the termination of persecution of Baha'is is still conditioned on their recanting their faith and they reportedly continue to be referred to as a "despised sect". According to the information received, the discrimination against members of the Baha'i community ranges from dismissal from employment, in particular government employment, invalidation of work permits, discontinuation of salary payment, orders to return salaries received as public employees, discontinuation of payment of pensions, confiscation of ration booklets, confiscation of property, expulsions from the university, refusal of admission to schools and universities, refusal of licences to open shops, to sentencing to improvement.

The government replied that "according to article 13 of the constitution of the Islamic Republic of Iran, Christians are considered as religious minorities and are free in performing their religious rituals and act in accordance with their canon law as far as their personal status and religious teachings are concerned". The supreme council of the cultural revolution, it added, "has authorized religious education according to the customs and language of religious minorities. Therefore any allegation in this respect is false."

As to rules for dress, the reply said "all women in Iran should observe the special dress prescribed by Islam". Girl students should thus wear the Islamic veil like other women. But the government denied that parents were forced to sign a promise that their daughters would wear the Islamic veil to school.

The case of the closing of the Iranian Bible Society "temporarily for wrongdoings and failing to respect the laws and regulations of the Islamic Republic of Iran" was before the court, the reply said, "and obviously after the issuance of the verdict and when the situation of the accused becomes clear, the society could continue its activities".

The reply made the following comments on the Baha'is:

> The number of Baha'is in the Islamic Republic of Iran is less than one thousand of the population. Muslim Ulamas have declared Baha'ism as a heresy.
>
> The centre of Baha'ism is located in Israel and is under the direct control of Zionism.
>
> Baha'is are enjoying the same rights as any other citizen in the Islamic Republic of Iran and no one is persecuted for being a Baha'i.

The reply admitted that "it might happen that some executive organs commit error or are reluctant to provide services to certain citizens" and that the government was willing to investigate all such cases brought to its notice.

A communication to the government of Israel asked about reports "that Israeli settlers in the West Bank have impeded the practice of religion by Muslim worshippers or have attacked their holy places and destroyed articles of worship".

The government reaffirmed Israel's policy of upholding religious freedom and the sanctity of religious sites, according to which "free access to places of worship is a cardinal principle". Since the beginning of the Palestinian uprising *(intifada)*, however, it said "extremists have exploited the special status of mosques and have turned them into instruments of the intifada. In many places, mosques and places of worship have become operational headquarters and centres for organizing, planning and inciting violent activity." As a result, the Israeli Defence Force had acted on several occasions.

To the question of whether article 306 of the penal code of Mauritania, which deals with apostasy, conforms with UN resolutions concerning intolerance and discrimination based on religion or belief, the government replied that freedom of belief is guaranteed and protected in Mauritania: "A person can embrace whatever beliefs he desires and no one can compel him to abandon or change those beliefs or prevent him from manifesting a faith." Article 306, it was explained, does not apply to persons who have not embraced the Islamic faith. The reply added:

> Apostasy from the Islamic religion, which guarantees so many freedoms and so much security, stability and social justice, is regarded as high treason and everyone is aware of the penalties that states impose for this type of offence, which threatens their stability and their very existence.... The precepts of this religion cannot be changed, since the holy law on which it is based comprises moral principles in which our society believes and any person who violates them arouses social indignation. Consequently apostasy constitutes one of the most serious offences against the public order and morality established by this religion.

In a communication to the government of Mexico, the Special Rapporteur referred to information received on the murder of two Protestant pastors by a group of Catholic fanatics, which, it was said, had "created a state of fear and insecurity among the country's Protestant community".

Describing the investigations and criminal proceedings against the alleged culprits, the reply said these murders in no way constituted government activities. "Pursuant to the Mexican constitution, there is complete freedom of thought, conscience and religion in Mexico. The freedom to profess one's religious belief and to practise the forms of worship inherent in a faith are protected by law."

By the time of his report the Special Rapporteur had not received a reply from the government of Nepal concerning allegations that Nepalese and foreign Christians had been subjected to "ill-treatment and discrimination in application of the Nepalese legal code which reportedly prescribes that no person shall disseminate Christianity, Islam or any other faith so as to disrupt the traditional religion of the Hindu community; the penalties are up to one year's imprisonment for conversion and between three and six years for dissemination." District police officials were reported to have detained Christians for long periods of time without formal charges, to have beaten Christians, to have demanded signing of confessions and to have attempted to force them to recant their faith.

The Special Rapporteur took up the allegations of persecution against the Ahmadis with the Pakistan government. "It has again been asserted that ordinance XX of 1984 prohibits Ahmadis from freely practising their faith, that they are not allowed to meet freely and for the past six years have not been authorized to hold their annual convention. It has also been reported that attacks against the Ahmadi community, including killing and destruction of villages, go unpunished." No reply was received from the government by the time of the report.

Allegations of religious discrimination against the Shi'a community were the subject of a communication to the government of Saudi Arabia. It was said that Shi'ites were not allowed to preach or practise some of their religious rites openly, such as the commemoration of the death of Imam Hussein, the Prophet's grandson, and that some were detained without charge or trial.

The government's reply insisted that there is no religious discrimination in Saudi Arabia and that the cases mentioned by the Special Rapporteur "relate to crimes and punishment of persons who went through legal procedures in accordance with the laws of the land applicable to all its inhabitants, native or non-native".

The Special Rapporteur took up with the Turkish government the case of Osman Coskun, an imam who was sentenced to sixteen years and eight months imprisonment for "anti-secular propaganda" and "membership of an anti-secular organization". He was reportedly punished for activities not in Turkey but as imam among Turks in the Federal Republic of Germany.

The reply noted that laicism is a fundamental tenet of the Turkish constitution and that the government believes

> laicism provides the basis for the true exercise of the right to freedom of religion and the prevention of discrimination based on religion... Mr Osman Coskun is one of those persons who aim to establish a theocratic Islamic state in Turkey. In 1980 he went to another European country with a view to propagating theocratic ideas among the large community of Turkish nationals existing in that country and to promoting organized activities to overthrow laicism in Turkey.

He was tried and sentenced under the Turkish penal code, the government said, "since his activities have been directed against the republic of Turkey".

The Special Rapporteur received no reply from the government of Vietnam about allegations concerning the arrest and trial of several Buddhist monks and Catholic priests because of their religious activities.

The absence of references to countries in Eastern Europe in the 1991 report (except Albania and Bulgaria) reflected a substantial improvement in the area of religious liberty in those countries, all of which had appeared prominently in earlier reports. The Special Rapporteur expressed gratification over "the radical changes in the enjoyment of the rights and freedoms of thought, conscience, religion or belief that have taken place in Eastern Europe".

What emerges from the Special Rapporteur's 1992 report is not much different, with practically all the forms of intolerance mentioned in the 1991 report being repeated. An overview of some of the cases may round out our picture.[2]

There was a communication with China about reports of government involvement being required in the search for the successor to the Panchen Lama, in apparent violation of ancient Tibetan Buddhist traditions that this spiritual leader is reincarnated in his successor. Cuba was asked about allegations of persecution of Jehovah's Witnesses. The case of a 12-year-old Iraqi native who was refused admission to a French state school "for wearing a head-scarf out of personal conviction" — although she had worn it in gymnastics classes for two years without a problem — was taken up with the government of France. An enquiry was made about provisions in Sudan's new criminal code stipulating the death penalty for apostasy from Islam.

Switzerland was asked about the prison sentence and fines imposed on a conscientious objector even though the military court acknowledged that his refusal to serve "was based on sincere religious belief" which created "a serious conflict of conscience". The Special Rapporteur asked the government of Saudi Arabia to comment on allegations that Islamic fasting regulations during Ramadan were also enforced on non-Muslims and that the importation of "non-Islamic religious material such as Christmas cards and Christmas trees" was outlawed.

The US government was asked whether a court decision (*Employment Division vs Smith*) upholding the dismissal of two drug rehabilitation counsellors who had taken peyote during a Native American religious ceremony did not "amount to a restriction of the right of indigenous people to practise their traditional religion". (We shall return to this case in chapter 4.)

Three instances of government responses cited by the Special Rapporteur offer further insights into how civil authorities in those countries understand religious freedom.

In a communication addressed to the government of Greece, the Special Rapporteur asked whether new procedures for the selection of Muftis introduced government interference "in the determination of religious representatives by the Muslim community", since they give the minister of national education and religious affairs the final choice, "which would make it an appointment rather than an election by the religious community itself".

The Greek government explained the law as follows:

> An enlarged committee is convened by the... competent regional secretary-general. This committee, chaired by the prefect, consists of Greek Muslim clergy and prominent Greek Muslim citizens. They propose to the minister of education and religious affairs a list of qualified persons. From among them the minister chooses on the basis of personal qualification of each candidate. The Mufti is finally appointed by presidential decree issued upon proposal by the minister of education.
>
> In this connection it should be recalled that the appointment by the state of a head of clergy is common practice in countries where Islam constitutes the predominant religion.

Greece is the unique Western country to accept the jurisdiction by a head of Muslim clergy.... The appointment through popular election would jeopardize the implementation of the constitutional requirements of assigning judges by law.

On 11 June 1991 the Special Rapporteur transmitted the following information to the government of Iraq:

According to information received, the Shi'a Muslim community in Iraq has been subjected over the past decade to various practices inconsistent with the provisions of the Declaration on the Elimination of All Forms of Intolerance and of Discrimination Based on Religion or Belief. In particular, it has been alleged that institutions of religious education have been systematically destroyed and religious leaders and scholars persecuted and killed.

The Special Rapporteur has received allegations that in the course of recent months the Shi'a community has suffered particular discrimination, and that an estimated 20,000 persons were recently killed in the cities of Karbala and Najaf within the framework of anti-government uprisings which had erupted among the Shi'a population at the end of the Gulf war... According to the sources, it is estimated that some 800 members of the clergy (300 teachers and 500 students) have recently been rounded up in the holy cities of Karbala and Najaf and are currently missing. It is feared that many have been executed.

In its extensive reply, the Iraqi government said it was "diligently endeavouring to preserve and develop religious centres with a view to promoting religious teachings and the humanitarian values that they comprise". As to the particular allegations, it said that

in the wake of the aggression by the coalition forces led by the United States of America, after the ceasefire some Iraqi towns fell prey to disturbances, consisting of acts of aggression against persons and official religious, social and educational institutions, as well as places of worship. The precious cultural and historical contents of those institutions, including religious and other manuscripts and books, were burnt and destroyed and innocent citizens were subjected to all forms of plunder, murder and sexual assault during those disturbances, which caused widespread devastation and a breakdown of public order and security, as a result of which the lives and property of citizens were threatened. The competent authorities fulfilled their duty by suppressing those disturbances and subversive acts in order to put an end to the state of anarchy, protect public order and security, and restore the rule of law and prevent any further violation thereof.

What actually happened in Karbala and Najaf, the government said, was that twenty clergymen and their families had sought refuge with the authorities and requested their protection from acts of sabotage. Insisting that the Iraqi government "has always treated the clergymen of all religious communities with all due respect for their religious and social status", the reply said clergymen in Najaf and Karbala "are still discharging their religious duties and leading completely normal lives without any harassment".

Thailand was approached by the Special Rapporteur about reports that the ministry of interior had issued arrest warrants for twelve leading members of the Unification Church, which is represented by the Unification Culture Foundation in Thailand. "Warrants were reportedly also issued for the arrest of the Reverend and Mrs Moon, should they come to the country, although they have not been accused of any violation of the law. It has been alleged that all Unification Church centres throughout the country have been raided. According to the sources, bail has repeatedly been denied for the persons who have already been imprisoned on the grounds that the movement they represent is a 'dangerous threat to the national security', although no formal charges have been brought against them."

The Thai government replied that these reports were inaccurate:

> The licence of the Unification Culture Foundation was revoked on 22 May 1991 at the request of the licensee, who was convinced that the Foundation, after its establishment, had engaged in inappropriate activities which were inconsistent with its original objectives, and as a result his own reputation was at stake. Some leaders of the Foundation were arrested on 26 June 1991 on charges of being accomplices to and supporting illegal activities, fraud and making false statements to the authorities. These charges are not related to religious beliefs, and they have full right of appeal to court.

Some concluding remarks from the 1992 report may serve as a useful summary of what this chapter has made clear about religious liberty:

The Special Rapporteur has continued to receive allegations of infringements of the rights and freedoms set out in the Declaration occurring in practically all regions of the world and is concerned at their persistence... The allegations concerning specific incidents of infringement of the rights and freedoms set out in the Declaration are not confined to a particular faith or geographical area. They range from extra-judicial killings of members of the clergy to the prohibition of certain specific manifestations relating to a particular religion or belief..[3]

NOTES

[1] Report on the *Implementation of the Declaration on the Elimination of All Forms of Intolerance and of Discrimination Based on Religon or Belief*, by the Special Rapporteur, Angelo Vidal d'Almeida Ribeiro, United Nations, Commission on Human Rights, January 1991. The specific instances quoted are on pp.60-117 of the report.

[2] Report on the *Implementation of the Declaration for the 1992 Session of the Commission on Human Rights*, C/CN.4/1992/52. The specific instances quoted are on pp.4-88 of the report.

[3] *Ibid*, pp.173-174.

3. Understanding Religious Liberty

> Everyone has the right to freedom of thought, conscience and religion; this right includes freedom to change his religion or belief, and freedom, either alone or in community with others and in public or private, to manifest his religion or belief in teaching, practice, worship and observance.
> *Universal Declaration of Human Rights*

While this is not a definition of religious liberty, it is widely accepted as a description of several elements of it. Given the difficulty of defining "religion", "freedom" and "liberty", it is not surprising that the term religious liberty is variously understood. Generally "religious freedom" and "religious liberty" are used synonymously, but some see the former as a broader concept and use the latter as a specific term to denote a political or legal right.

Canada's new Charter of Rights and Freedoms simply guarantees "religious freedom", while China's constitution stipulates that "citizens enjoy freedom of religious belief". Whether freedom of religious belief is something less than religious freedom is an interesting question.

What makes religious liberty complex and difficult to define is the presence of different actors, among them individuals, religious bodies, the larger community and the state. The interactions among these, which may differ from context to context, shape and influence the understanding, scope and extent of religious liberty.

In his work on the ecumenical discussions of religious liberty Carillo de Albornoz makes a helpful division of four aspects of religious liberty: liberty of conscience, liberty of religious expression, liberty of religious association and corporate and institutional religious freedom.[1] Only the first, which some would call "absolute religious liberty", is, according to Carillo, "pure religious liberty". The other aspects are qualified or dependent on broader human rights.

It is significant that the Universal Declaration of Human Rights speaks of the "freedom of thought, conscience and religion" all together. But these rights also extend to those who do not profess a religion. Their thought and conscience enjoy the same freedom.

Freedom of conscience and freedom of religion are sometimes used synonymously. On the basis of the liberty of conscience a strong argument can be made that people should be allowed to act on the basis of their religious convictions and should not be coerced to alter those convictions. Long before any civil protection was accorded to religious liberty, Little points out, the struggle between conscience and state, between the "internal forum" and the "external forum", or between the "sword of the spirit" and the "sword of steel", persisted.[2] John Calvin placed freedom of conscience at the centre of his theological concerns. He emphasized the distinction between the inner forum or the forum of conscience and the earthly forum or human government.

Conscience is the focal point of religious liberty in a classic work on the subject by M. Searle Bates. He writes: "Conscience is the essence of the matter — responsible first to God, to truth, to duty rather than to government, to a human authority in a religious body or to opinion. Respect for conscience runs through all effort to secure religious liberty... the true quality of conscience is actually significant in the field of religion, broadly considered as man's devotion to supreme values."[3] Others disagree. Jay Newman argues that "however important 'conscience' may be in relation to religious liberty, it is not the 'essence' of the matter and has been dangerously overvalued by proponents of religious liberty". This is because "conscience" can be understood in any number of ways: "primarily a source of moral knowledge, primarily a force that encourages or discourages them from doing certain things or primarily a source of guilt after the deed".[4] Moreover, it has been recognized that conscience is fallible and subject to error.

In any case, it is clear that religious convictions are part of the inner spiritual freedom of a human being. To the believer it is that spiritual freedom which ensures direct communication between the human being and God. This inner freedom is the internal aspect of religious liberty. The external manifestations of that inner freedom require political rights and privileges — the external or social aspect of religious liberty. These external aspects can include the observance of religious customs and ceremonies, belonging to an association or body of religious believers, expressing and acting out of religious commitment, teaching and propagating the belief. What is generally understood as religious liberty is the freedom for such external manifestations.

One may argue that spiritual or inner freedom can be maintained irrespective of the external aspects, but most religions would maintain that the fullness of such inner freedom is expressed only through its external manifestations. In that sense, religious belief is not a private affair. But the internal freedom is the core, and it may be claimed as absolute. However, this internal aspect is not entirely free of external conditions. Unfortunately, even this internal liberty can be restricted by external factors. A state may coerce a citizen to profess values or beliefs which he or she does not hold. But this possibility cannot deny the claim that this aspect of inner freedom should be pure or absolute.

This distinction between inner freedom and external conditions is important in examining the affirmation that there is a distinctive Christian basis for religious liberty. Jacques Ellul insists that "Christianity carries with it the proclamation of religious freedom, for when the church and Christianity reject religious freedom they deny themselves. They do not speak the word they are charged to speak. They ruin their message and Christ's own work. When the church denies this freedom, it destroys its own freedom."[5] It can be maintained that the universality of the mission of the church implies and demands religious liberty. Inherent in the Christian gospel is a mandate to propagate it. That was the mission assigned to the disciples by Jesus Christ, and it cannot be fulfilled without religious liberty.

But when Christians seek a doctrinal basis for religious liberty, it is usually linked to their understanding of spiritual freedom and inherent human dignity. Freedom, which is the gift of the Holy Spirit, is at the centre of the Christian faith. "For freedom Christ has set us free. Stand firm, therefore, and do not submit again to a yoke of slavery" (Gal. 5:1). It can be argued that freedom is integral to Christian teaching about the nature of the human person. The WCC's Amsterdam assembly expressed the inter-relationship between the inner Christian freedom with which Christ has set us free and social or external religious freedom: "While the liberty with which Christ has set men free can neither be given nor destroyed by any government, Christians, because of that inner freedom, are both jealous for its outward expression and solicitous that all men should have freedom in religious life."

Inner freedom is not subject to any laws or restraints. Given by God, it cannot be destroyed by the state. But as we have said, state coercion can distort the exercise of even the inner freedom. This intertwining of internal freedom and external freedom does not mean religious liberty as a political right is the same as inner freedom; but inner freedom demands external expression, and religious freedom must therefore be jealously guarded.

St Paul points out in Romans 8 that inner freedom can remain despite outward tyranny. Wogaman takes up this issue:

> Christians following Paul believe that salvation and spiritual freedom can occur under even the most totalitarian circumstances, a proposition which has undergone successful test on numerous occasions through the centuries... But life is social. Salvation pertains to a quality of relationship with God, and it issues in a kind of relationship with other persons. The full richness of Christian life must be actualized in the context of society, in words and deeds bearing witness to the relationship with God. Unless man is externally free to bear witness to God, the inner intention of the covenant between God and man remains frustrated.[6]

Orthodox scholar John Romanides argues that

> the idea that religious liberty is necessary for the expression of inner Christian freedom or faith is from an Orthodox point of view absolutely wrong. Religious liberty is no doubt a human right and a wonderful thing to have, if this be the will of God in any given situation, but martyrdom is after all one of the best and in many cases the highest expression of one's inner Christian freedom. To remain faithful in one's love of God in the face of persecution or any kind of suffering and to be willing to forgo one's own salvation and well-being for that of others is an expression of non-utilitarian love or inner Christian freedom.[7]

Most Christian thinkers, however, hold the view that the extent of religious liberty determines the expression of inner Christian freedom and that religious liberty is thus not a luxury but a basic need. A bishop in a country which was then under Marxist rule once told me his church had religious liberty because it had "freedom for the eucharist". When pressed, he admitted that this is not sufficient, because to live out the meaning of eucharist, the "liturgy after the liturgy", more freedom was needed.

Narrowing the concept of religious liberty to inner freedom may reflect a divorce of religion from the larger life of society, politics and economics. Religion then becomes privatized. Because such compartmentalization between the "sacred" and the "secular" is not acceptable, religious liberty must be broad enough to include its implications in and for society.

The status of the human person as created, redeemed and called by God, including his or her destiny and vocation, is characterized by freedom. Carillo de Albornoz calls it "an essential characteristic of the gospel that God himself does not use force to win our allegiance. And this divine respect for human freedom is a revelation, directed decisively at the world, about the source and meaning of power, for even the state and its coercive power exists by virtue of the love and power of God, who does not compel faith."[8]

But it is not only churches and Christian organizations, but also the United Nations and secular organizations, who affirm that the basis of religious liberty (like other human rights) is the inherent dignity of the human person — though *why* the human person possesses the inherent dignity to justify a claim to such rights is not always made explicit.

Victor Conde argues that a solid theological basis for this claim is necessary. "If such 'inherent dignity' is merely a human anthropological value judgment, albeit universal, it is weak indeed, as history has manifested. If, however, such dignity comes from a source above mankind, and if that source is universal, absolute and immutable, then such rights based on such dignity could, if respected, survive the vicissitudes of often fickle legal systems in fallen man's fickle hands."[9]

God is the giver of the inherent human dignity. That human beings are made in the image of God is central to the biblical account of creation. The dignity implanted at creation has been reaffirmed in the incarnation and redemption by Jesus Christ. Swiss theologian Thorwald Lorenzen says: "If Christ is God's self-revelation and if he was fully human, then in the Christ-event the divine dignity of human nature has been established by God."

Lorenzen draws several important consequences from this theological observation. First, all people are equal in the sight of God. This is not only the message of the creation accounts but also the New Testament conviction that it is God's will for all people to be saved. Second, God is related to all his creatures and can speak through unexpected channels. "By granting liberty to all men the Christian is giving concrete expression to his expectancy that God may work in diverse ways."[10] Third, each human being should be free in relation to God. That relationship, which should not be circumscribed by others, becomes the basis for one's relationships with other human beings, even if this is not acknowledged. Freedom in these relationships is the essence of religious freedom.

> Man is a dialogical being, meant to dialogue with both man and God. True dialogue presupposes freedom, openness and voluntariness. Just as God grants man the liberty to reject his love, so man, for the sake of possibility of dialogue, will grant religious liberty to others... Any use of force or pressure — either political, economic, or psychological — to attain religious adherence is a misunderstanding of faith. Faith can only originate and grow in an atmosphere of voluntary response. The Christian cannot deny to others what God gives to all, i.e. the liberty to believe or not to believe.

The WCC's Amsterdam assembly said freedom of religion is an essential element to a good international order — an implication it drew from "the Christian faith and the worldwide nature of Christianity". Amsterdam laid down four basic rights: (1) to determine one's own faith and creed; (2) to express one's religious beliefs in worship, teaching and practice and to proclaim them to others; (3) to associate and organize with others for religious purposes; and (4) the right of religious organizations to determine policies and practices for accomplishing their purposes. Religious liberty exists where these rights can be freely exercised. Obviously, there can be degrees of religious liberty.

This formulation may be understood as implying that these rights are granted or restricted by some external authority or that the exercise of some or all of these rights is permitted or tolerated. A distinction may be drawn between genuine religious liberty and religious tolerance. The absence of religious intolerance is conducive to religious liberty but it does not guarantee it. While the term "tolerance" has frequently been used from the standpoint of the majority community, it has often been the legal guarantee of religious liberty for all. Gladstone said "religious toleration requires that civil penalty or prohibition be not employed to punish or to preclude a man's acting on his own religious opinion... It requires that no privilege or benefit which a person is capable of receiving rightly and of using beneficially be withheld from him on account of his religious opinion as such."[11] Although it is difficult to define the difference precisely, it must be conceded that tolerance is less than liberty. This is important to note because the terms "tolerance" and "intolerance" are increasingly used in international discussion of religious liberty.

The difficulty in defining religious liberty is compounded by the diverse claims that have been made by individuals and groups in the name of religious liberty. Too much has gone by the name of religion, and too many things have been done in the name of religion. The external aspects of religious liberty thus cannot be absolute, but must be seen in relation to other human rights and the human rights of all in a society.

Religious liberty is generally listed prominently in any compilation of human rights. Expansion of the understanding of religious liberty has usually taken place when the scope of human rights as a whole has broadened. For a variety of reasons religious liberty occupies a unique and distinctive place among human rights.

In modern times perhaps the most striking statement of the place of religious freedom alongside other fundamental freedoms was by President Franklin D. Roosevelt in an address to the US Congress on 6 January 1941:

> In the future days which we seek to make secure, we look forward to a world founded upon four essential human freedoms.
>
> The first is freedom of speech and expression — everywhere in the world. The second is freedom of every person to worship God in his own way — everywhere in the world. The third is freedom from want — which, translated into world terms, means economic undertakings which will secure to every nation a healthy peacetime life for its inhabitants — everywhere in the world. The fourth is freedom from fear — which, translated into world terms, means a worldwide reduction of armaments to such a point and in such a thorough fashion that no nation will be in a position to commit an

act of physical aggression against any neighbour — anywhere in the world... Freedom means the supremacy of human rights everywhere.

It is significant that Roosevelt not only emphasized the universal nature of human rights but anticipated the next generation of human rights. "Traditional freedoms of speech and of worship should go hand in hand with such wider human rights as economic and social welfare and peace and security for all peoples and persons. Roosevelt perceived human rights in a broad and comprehensive manner, particularly by relating them to international peace and development and by stressing their universal scope."[12]

The universality and fundamental nature of religious liberty lead often to the claim that the most fundamental freedom is religious freedom. Indeed, some national constitutions affirm the primacy of religious freedom among fundamental rights. In the Bill of Rights appended to the US Constitution, religious liberty is clearly the first freedom. In Canada's Charter of Rights and Freedoms, "freedom of religion" is the first freedom acknowledged. Newman sees "historical warrant for treating religious liberty as the 'first' freedom, conceptually as well as chronologically".[13]

The WCC's third assembly (New Delhi, 1961) asserted that religious freedom is a distinctive human right: "Holding a distinctive Christian basis for religious liberty, we regard this right as fundamental for men everywhere." As Carillo points out, "the New Delhi assembly is dealing with the Christian view of human rights. To be a distinctive or a unique human right means that religious liberty is not merely the application of the common human rights to religious matters or activities, but that it is a human right specifically different from the others, with its own peculiar notions and contents."[14]

The claim that the religious sphere is different from and superior to other human activities and the implication that special considerations have to be given in applying general human rights to the religious sphere may not be accepted by those outside the religious sphere or the external authorities who decide on the application of human rights.

But that does not make the claim invalid. The substance of religious liberty *is* different from other freedoms. At the "absolute" or "pure" level, religious liberty is about the human being's relation with the divine. Carillo argues that the "essential transcendency of the human relationship with God fully justifies... the consideration of religious liberty as a distinctive and unique human right".[15]

This special quality puts religious liberty on a different level from other human rights, leading to the general perception that violations of religious liberty are more serious than violations of other human rights. In no way does this imply special privileges for the church or any other religious body. Religious rights are equally and universally applicable. The religious freedom of any person or group is not an unbridled freedom which might serve as a pretext for violating the freedoms of others. The distinctive nature of religious liberty is conceptual, not a matter of special claims. Its primacy lies in having a transcendent dimension which other rights do not have.

Newman sees evidence that there is "something primal" about religious liberty in its close customary association with freedom of conscience and freedom of thought, "even though conscience and thought are not in fact necessarily related to religion".[16] But the exercise of religious liberty involves and is intertwined with all other human rights as well. Religious liberty is not an isolated right. Freedom is comprehensive and indivisible in principle; it cannot be fragmented without jeopardy to the whole. Religious liberty exists or is denied in the midst of a complex set of institutions and human rights. It is sustained by other liberties and cannot be exercised without them. Historically, the effort to secure religious liberty has been successful only when associated with other liberties; and successful struggles for religious liberty have promoted and enhanced several other civil liberties, in particular freedom of expression and freedom of association.

In the exercise of religious liberty, greater claims are usually made in the name of freedom of expression and freedom of association. It may be argued that, because religious expression is both free exercise of religion and free speech, it is more fully protected than ordinary speech. Not everyone will accept such a claim. Others will argue that religious expression is neither more nor less than ordinary speech and that there cannot be distinctions in the treatment of free speech. This is partly because of the general understanding that freedom of speech should not be normally limited and that this applies to religious speech also. Some limitations may be necessary, for speech or writing can cause damage to others and imperil the community and religious speech may cause even greater harm than other speeches. But still the authorities have to show enough evidence to put any limits.

The *fatwa* issued by the late Ayatollah Khomeini against the author Salman Rushdie raised a number of questions related to religious belief and freedom of expression, in addition to the question of the universally accepted right to life. This decree instructed Muslims to seek out and kill Salman Rushdie for writing the book *Satanic Verses*, which the ayatollah and his followers considered blasphemous. A price of 1.5 million pounds was placed on his head, and the threat and reward were endorsed by the governmental authorities in Iran. Rushdie went into hiding and still remains in hiding.

Kevin Boyle, director of the International Centre on Censorship, Article 19, contends that the *Satanic Verses* issue does not involve a conflict between freedom of religion and freedom of expression. "The issue is rather how far does respect for the beliefs of others extend? It is respect for other people's beliefs that is at issue. There is no place for a holy war on behalf of any religion or creed, and no justification for forcing a writer to take refuge in fear of his life." Freedom of expression, Boyle says, includes the freedom to doubt the truth of any belief.[17]

With regard to freedom of association and corporate freedom, a religious institution serving explicitly religious ends is generally granted more rights and privileges than, for example, an economic institution such as a business corporation.

The exercise of religious liberty involves other human rights as well. Among these is the right to physical and mental integrity of the human person, freedom from arbitrary arrest and detention, freedom to leave one's country and to return to it, freedom of education. Indeed, many aspects of religious liberty have little or no meaning if other human rights are not effectively ensured. Religious liberty gets its full meaning only in the broad context of human rights; and violations of religious liberty are often accompanied by gross violations of human rights or even crimes against humanity such as genocide.

NOTES

[1] A.F. Carillo de Albornoz, *The Basis of Religious Liberty*, London, SCM, 1963, p.22.
[2] David Little, John Kelsay & Abdulaziz Sachedina, *Human Rights and the Conflict of Cultures*, Columbia, SC, University of South Carolina Press, 1988, p.15.
[3] M. Searle Bates, *Religious Liberty, an Inquiry*, New York/London, International Missionary Council, 1945, p.373.
[4] Jay Newman, *On Religious Freedom*, Toronto, University of Toronto Press, 1991, p.127.
[5] Jacques Ellul, *The Ethics of Freedom*, Grand Rapids, MI, Eerdmans, 1976, pp.443-444.
[6] Philip Wogaman, *Protestant Faith and Religious Liberty*, Nashville, TN, Abingdon Press, 1967, p.65.
[7] John S. Romanides, "The Orthodox Churches on Church-State Relations and Religious Liberty", in *Readings on Church and State*, ed. James E. Wood Jr, Waco, TX, J.M. Dawson Institute of Church-State Studies, 1989, p.259.
[8] Carillo de Albornoz, *op. cit.*, p.82.
[9] H. Victor Conde, "The Theological Basis of Human Rights", *C.L.S. Quarterly*, vol. v, no. 3, p.10.
[10] Thorwald Lorenzen, "The Theological Basis for Religious Liberty", *Journal of Church and State*, vol. 21, no. 3, 1979, p.420.
[11] William Gladstone, quoted in A.R. Vidler, *The Orb and the Cross*, London, SPCK, 1945, pp.117-118.
[12] Theo van Boven, "Religious Liberty in the Context of Human Rights", *The Ecumenical Review*, vol. 37, no. 3, 1985, p.347.
[13] Newman, *op. cit.*, p.99.
[14] Carillo de Albornoz, *op. cit.*, p.36.
[15] *Ibid.*, p.37.
[16] Newman, *op. cit.*, p.100.
[17] Kevin Boyle, "Freedom of Religion, Freedom of Expression — Salman Rushdie Case", *Conscience and Liberty*, vol. 1, no. 3, 1990, pp.84-85.

4. Religious Liberty and the State

In the dramatic aftermath of a revolt against the British government in India, Queen Victoria made the following declaration on religious freedom in 1858:

> Firmly relying ourselves on the truth of Christianity and acknowledging with gratitude the solace of religion, we disclaim alike the right and desire to impose our convictions on any of our subjects, but declare it to be our royal will and pleasure that none be in any wise favoured, or molested or disquieted by reason of their religious faith or observances, but that all shall alike enjoy the equal and impartial protection of the law; and we do strictly charge and enjoin all those who may be in authority under us that they abstain from all interference with religious belief or worship of any of our subjects on pain of our highest displeasure.

This declaration is a reminder that while religious freedom may claim theological and moral motivations, as we saw in the previous chapter, the exercise of it is a resolutely social and judicial matter and is generally decided by the state. The nature of a state, its constitution and laws have a direct bearing on religious liberty. When constitutions and laws change, the extent of religious liberty may be expanded or restricted. The state is therefore the main actor on the scene of religious liberty in the modern period.

The common understanding that religious liberty is determined by church-state relations is a useful shorthand for discussing many current problems, but "church-state" terminology is in fact inadequate. It arises from the situation in Europe and had its origin at a time when the church was monolithic and governmental power was centred in a single ruler. Many religions do not have the kind of organized structures found in the Christian church. Some states are based on particular religions, making the distinction between religion and state difficult. It is more accurate to say that religious liberty is dependent on the relation between religions, including their organized structures, and the state, in the sense of political authority.

When we think of religious liberty we usually have in mind the rights or privileges granted to us and our fellows or otherwise acknowledged to belong to us and our fellows by existing political or civil authority. Thus H.G. Wood describes religious liberty as "primarily a demand on the state to secure to the individual citizen and to organized religious groups certain rights. In a genuinely democratic state, the government is asked to protect the responsible adult citizen in holding and professing whatever ultimate beliefs commend themselves to his conscience and reason."[1]

Because of the key role played by the state in religious liberty, it is useful to look more closely at the state. In popular parlance "state" and "government" are used synonymously. It is more precise to say that the state functions through the government. Every citizen belongs to a state but not to a government. Many countries make a constitutional distinction between the head of state and the head of government. State represents something wider than the government. While the state continues, the government changes.

The state is the institution in which the ultimate political authority and power necessary to maintain order and to provide conscious direction to the life of a society are located. As with many other human rights, it is assumed that the authority which provides or determines religious liberty is legitimate. If a government is not considered politically or morally legitimate, the denial of rights may become an additional ground for opposition. Traditionally, the legitimacy of a government was very much linked to how it came to power. This notion has undergone change in the modern period. The crucial test is accountability to the people. Moral legitimacy may be gained, maintained or lost by a government.

In discussions of the Christian understanding of state, perhaps the most often quoted biblical passage is Romans 13:1: "Let every person be subject to the governing authorities; for there is no authority except from God, and those authorities that exist have been instituted by God." Not surprisingly, this has been a favourite passage of rulers, including some who have used it against politically active churches and Christian individuals. In this passage Paul sets the state within God's design on earth. For Paul, and the earliest Christians, the political realm was in itself a manifestation of God on earth which required submission and obedience. This reflected an early concept of the state which has largely broken down. Today the moral legitimacy of a state is more and more determined by its actions and policies rather than by any divine authorization.

If Paul offers one concept of state in the letter to the Romans, another picture is drawn in the book of Revelation (13:1-18). Here the picture is of a state which has lost all its legitimacy, reflecting the reality that it is within the nature of power to be tempted to exceed its bounds and to demand total allegiance and obedience from human beings. The apocalyptic beast expressly represents the Roman empire, with its cult of the emperor, but implicitly the subject is every political regime of any era which takes on a totalitarian aspect. At that point it is not the state but resistance to the state which is legitimate.

But there is a third passage from the New Testament that is also appropriate to a discussion of religious liberty: the well-known words of Jesus to the Pharisees: "Give therefore to the emperor the things that are the emperor's, and to God the things that are God's" (Matt. 22:21). The background of this statement is important. In an effort to force Jesus to say something that would get him in trouble, the Pharisees asked: "Is it lawful to pay taxes to the emperor, or not?" Jesus asked them to produce the coin used for the tax and gave his reply looking at the image of Caesar on the coin. Jesus' answer was not just a clever diplomatic way out of a tight spot. Obviously he did not fall into the trap. Instead, he used the occasion to state a cardinal principle: the state — here personified in the emperor — can claim only what belongs to it. The coin has the emperor's image; that belongs to him. A human being has the image of God and belongs to God. Ultimate loyalty can only be to God. The emperor cannot claim it or inhibit its expression. The state does not have unlimited authority from God; it is not entitled to rule over the conscience of human beings. A human person, Bates says, "created, redeemed and called by God and as God intends to deal with him, is responsible solely to God... Therefore the state, which is subordinated to God's authority and laws, must respect this human responsibility before God. Consequently, religious liberty would not be ultimately based on the limitation of political authority, but inversely the latter would flow from the freedom which God has given man."[2]

Various attempts have been made to classify the different "models" of church-state relationship which have had some

importance in different places at different times. Philip Wogaman's typology suggests four basic types:
- Theocracy: the state is under the control of religious leaders or institutions for religious purposes.
- Erastianism: the church under the control of the state has been termed "Erastianism" (after the sixteenth-century Swiss German Thomas Erastes).
- Separation of church and state — friendly: religious and political institutions are legally separate but not hostile to each other.
- Separation of church and state — unfriendly: religious and political institutions are legally separate and in an antagonistic relationship.[3]

This useful typology needs several qualifications. The term "theocracy" itself is debatable; etymologically, its meaning is "rule by God". In practice the reference is usually to a situation in which the state is under the control of religious leaders or institutions — of which there have been many examples in history. In the contemporary world both Iran and Israel are often cited as examples of theocratic states — which in itself reveals the complexity of the issue, given the great differences between them. The nature of the government of Iran (since the overthrow of the shah) is very much dependent on a particular understanding of state and society by Islam. Some scholars have raised doubts about whether a constitutional Islamic state can be a theocratic one. The case of Israel is perhaps even more complex. Here the "theocratic" dimension emerges more from the theological justification of the state than from its constitution.

The second type, "Erastianism", also covers a variety of situations. If it is used to refer to the use of the church or religion by the state, then it has characterized all sorts of governments all throughout history. State authorities almost invariably try to coopt religion. A more precisely defined category is the "established church". There are states which have an official religion or church. Such establishment, often part of the constitution, raises a number of issues related to religious liberty. The established church may enjoy privileges and therefore rights which other churches or religions do not have. In English law, as the debate on Salman Rushdie showed, blasphemy law is applicable only to Christianity and specifically to the Church of England. But at the same time as it enjoys greater privileges, the established church may not have full freedom, since many decisions about it are made by organs of the state. The real test in situations where there is an established church is the extent to which religious liberty is enjoyed by other churches and religions.

In a 1986 study, Elizabeth Odio Benito, the Special Rapporteur of the UN Commission on Human Rights, listed eight arrangements between state and church:[4]
— State religions
— Established churches
— Neutral or secular as regards religion
— No official religion
— Separation of church from state
— Arrangements with the Roman Catholic Church
— Protection of legally recognized religious groups
— Millet system, recognizing a number of religious communities.

It is widely accepted that separation of church and state is more conducive to religious freedom than other types. But several considerations are relevant here. Separation, as Wogaman notes, can be unfriendly, hostile, antagonistic. Constitutional provisions of separation may mean mere toleration of religion or even legal prevention of organized interference by religion in the affairs of the state. It may result in indifference of the state in religious affairs. It may assume that the state has no obligation to promote religious values which may contribute to the common good of the state as a whole. Of course, separation of church and state in a democratic state and separation in a totalitarian state can be very different, since religious liberty, as we have seen, is intertwined with other rights which are more secure within a democratic system.

The sixteenth-century Anabaptists were among the first to champion religious liberty in the modern sense and to describe church-state relations that would ensure such liberty. At the time, Estep notes, "thought patterns were enmeshed in, and determined by, the traditional medieval framework of the holy Roman empire. Neither civil nor church leaders could ordinarily conceive of a stable society that did not unite church and state *(corpus Christianum)*. And yet the Anabaptists' view of the state was to prove their most far-reaching contribution to the modern world."[5]

The Anabaptist participants in the Bern Disputation of 1538 made one of the earliest systematic statements of the concept of the separation of church and state: "We grant that in the non-Christian world the state authorities have a legitimate place, to keep order, to punish the evil and to protect the good. But we as Christians live according to the gospel and our only authority and Lord is Jesus Christ. Christians consequently do not use the sword, which is worldly, but they use the Christian ban."

Basically it was the Anabaptist understanding of the nature of the church that made them insist on the separation of church and state. The church can be free under God only when it is separate from the state. That was necessary for religious freedom. Thus the Anabaptists became the first champions of religious liberty.

It was the United States which for the first time institutionalized separation of church and state through clear constitutional provisions. It was enunciated in the form of the first amendment to its new constitution in 1791. The first sixteen words of the Bill of Rights — "Congress shall make no law respecting an establishment of religion, or prohibiting the free exercise thereof..." — became the most influential constitutional provision for religious liberty ever enacted. The first amendment did not actually *decree* separation of church and state; it *assumed* it. The free exercise of religion and non-establishment of churches were conceivable because of a prior conception of church and state as separate institutions operating in distinct spheres. While the first amendment has determined two centuries of judicial history in the United States, it has also inspired the thinking on church-state relations in many parts of the world and the international discourse on religious liberty.

The Williamsburg Charter, a celebration and reaffirmation of the religious liberty clauses drafted by representatives of America's leading faiths for the bicentennial of the Bill of Rights, says:

> The first amendment is a momentous decision for religious liberty, the most important political decision for religious liberty and public justice in the history of humankind. Limitation upon religious liberty is allowable only where the state has borne a heavy burden of proof that the limitation is justified — not by any

ordinary public interest, but by a supreme public necessity — and that no less restrictive alternative to limitation exists.[6]

The passage of the first amendment climaxed a long period of colonial history in which church-state relations were tested. The English colonization of North America was too complex to attribute to any single factor, but it is widely accepted that religion played an important part. Missionary and religious purposes are highlighted in practically all statements of purposes and in every charter issued.

However, not all of these early settlers who were so vitally interested in the advancement of religion believed in freedom of religion. Robert T. Miller points out the paradox of "the extreme intolerance of many..., particularly the settlers of New England, who had only recently fled... to escape persecution. Freedom of religion meant freedom only for their own particular concepts and practices."[7] The great exception was Rhode Island, where Roger Williams propounded religious freedom and complete separation of church and state.

The formulation of the US constitutional principle on religious liberty was mainly the work of Thomas Jefferson and James Madison, whose thinking grew out of the European Enlightenment. Two different metaphors used by Jefferson and Madison reflect the scope and limits of the first amendment. In a 1 January 1802 letter to the Danbury (Connecticut) Baptist Association, Thomas Jefferson wrote that he "contemplated with sovereign reverence that act of the whole American people which declared that their legislature should 'make no law respecting an establishment of religion, or prohibiting the free exercise thereof', thus building a *wall of separation* between church and state". Thirty years later Madison wrote that he had to "admit... that it may not be easy, in every possible case, to trace the *line of separation* between the rights of religion and the civil authority with such distinctness as to avoid collisions and doubts on unessential points".

It is obvious that "line of separation" is a more accurate phrase than "wall of separation". The latter has created a lot of confusion and conflict. The separation is less a wall sealing off two spheres than a shifting line tracking the rough boundaries within which the two institutions move and work. The metaphor of a line also takes into account possible evolutions of the two institutions.

A state in which there is separation of religion and state is usually referred to as a secular state. Secularism as a state policy has often been promoted as a guarantee for religious liberty and equality among religions. But in recent years this concept has run into heavy weather. In many newly independent and emerging states, secularization was presented along with modernization as part of a package for development. The distinction between secularization and secularism was not often maintained. Reaction against secularization, especially in the context of religious renaissance, has reopened the discussion of the secular state in some countries.

Indeed, statements on religious liberty by religious groups often reveal a defensive attitude vis-a-vis the state, depicting it as an actual or potential aggressor of freedom of religion against which one must defend human rights. This is understandable since religious liberty is so much dependent on the state and there are all too many instances of assaults on religious freedom by states. However, defensiveness does not solve the complex and intricate question of the state's competence concerning religious activities.

Separation of church and state implies that the state has no competence — and therefore no power — to judge or define religious truths. The problem arises when the state tries to decide what are religious activities and what are not. For example, in expelling the Christian Conference of Asia (CCA) in 1987, the Singapore government said some of the activities of the regional ecumenical organization were not religious. To the government, CCA's engagement in human rights struggles was political; the CCA understood this as religious, part of the very mission of the church.

When the Singapore government introduced the Maintenance of Religious Harmony Bill in January 1990, claiming that it was meant to prevent religious zealots from creating strife and political subversives from exploiting religions, the issue of separation between religion and politics was debated again. The Roman Catholic archdiocese of Singapore described the separation of politics and religion as a "complex and problematic proposal" which could cause confusion if "politics" was not carefully defined. If defined narrowly to mean party politics, it was acceptable to say that, in Singapore, no religion should espouse the cause of any political party and politics should be left to lay people — including lay Catholics. But when "politics" is used to mean "the study and practice of public affairs", it is akin to religion in that it affects the whole of human life. "To say that religion and politics can be separated is, at best, an ambiguous statement."

In the continuing definitional struggle between religion and politics, each side feels that the other is encroaching upon its domain. What may be claimed as legitimate religious activities by a religious body or an individual may be considered political activity by the state. This debate has arisen sharply in recent years in many countries besides Singapore.

It can be said that the duty of the state is not only to recognize and respect religious freedom but also to protect it against the many extra-legal forces which tend to hinder it or destroy it. The state can and should take impartial measures to ensure conditions under which religious institutions can live and grow. But there are several reasons why a state may be particularly sensitive about claims in the area of religious liberty. Because religion implies a belief in a higher authority than the state, religious liberty opens the way to the teaching and practice of ideas which may call into question the nature and policy of the state. Moreover, many religions by nature function in an organized form. Unless religion is banned (as was done in Albania in 1967) even in the absence of a civil society the church may be functioning as an organization. Even in a tightly-controlled society, the church is always an implicit and sometimes an explicit political force. Indeed, its political profile may be even higher in a more repressive society.

All states put some limitations on religious liberty as a general rule and sometimes severe ones under special circumstances. Some such constitutional and legal limitations on religious liberty may be justifiable and even necessary. No liberty is absolute and any liberty, even religious liberty, can be misused. Like other freedoms, religious liberty should not be allowed to be used irresponsibly; and it is within the state's competence to ensure that misuse of freedom is not allowed.

Here, too, there are serious problems. It is one thing to agree in general that some limitations on religious liberty are legitimate and necessary, quite another to agree on exactly which limitations are legitimate or necessary.

Among limitations on religious freedom acknowledged in ecumenical statements cited by Carillo de Albornoz are such formulations as "maintenance of public order and security", "defence of morals and public order", "maintaining law and order for the well-being of all", "public order, health and morality".[8]

Terms like these are used by many constitutions to describe the limits of religious freedom. Admittedly they are vague and subject to various interpretations. They have often been misused by states in an onslaught on religious freedom. But in spite of the vagueness, elasticity and potential misinterpretations the usefulness of the concepts cannot be disputed.

The WCC's Amsterdam Assembly recognized some limits:

a) The liberty of conscience, or right to determine one's belief is practically subject to no legal limitation at all.
b) The liberty of religious expression is subject to such limitations, prescribed by law as are necessary to protect order and welfare, morals and the rights and freedoms of others.
c) The liberty of religious association is subject to the same limits imposed on all associations by non-discriminatory laws.
d) Similarly, the corporate religious freedom is limited by the provisions of non-discriminatory laws passed in the interest of public order and well-being.

In other words, freedom of conscience is absolute and other aspects of religious freedom are closely linked to general human rights and subject to any reasonable limits on them. Some, however, would maintain with regard to religious liberty that the other aspects, too, have a special dimension and should enjoy greater protection than their related general human rights.

Among the qualifying provisions used by constitutions to limit religious liberty is that found in the Chinese constitution. An article in *Beijing Review* notes that "the religious freedom that Chinese citizens enjoy under the constitution and the law entertains obligations stipulated by the same. The constitution makes it clear that no one shall make use of religion to engage in activities to disrupt public order, impair the health of citizens or interfere with the state's educational system."[9] The reference here to the state's educational system is significant, since education has been a subject of controversy between church and state in many countries.

It is evident that certain expressions of religion and organized religious activities can be harmful to the society and may disturb peace and order. But the application of laws in this context should not be decided arbitrarily by the state, but should be the subject of a continuing dialogue among civil authorities, religious groups and other interested parties.

Interpretations by courts of even well-defined constitutional provisions ensuring religious liberty may change. We referred in passing in chapter 2 to the judgment by the US Supreme Court in the case of *Employment Division vs Smith*.

In April 1990 the Supreme Court ruled that the state of Oregon was justified in denying unemployment benefits to two American Indians who had lost their jobs as drug counsellors because they had participated in a religious ceremony which involved the ingesting of the mild hallucinogenic drug peyote, which is prohibited by Oregon law. This judgment, and especially the reasons given for it, disturbed many concerned with religious liberty. The Supreme Court was petitioned to reconsider its decision by an improbable alliance of Protestant fundamentalists, the American Civil Liberties Union, Mormons, Southern Baptists and liberal Jews. The judgment seemed to reject the well-established principle that government should not restrict or burden religious practice unless it was necessary to serve a "compelling" state interest. In this case, the argument by the majority of the justices was that the exercise of religion deserves no special protection, so long as the law or regulation impinging on it is "neutral" and generally applicable. The Court held that only laws "specially directed" at religion are laws "prohibiting" free exercise, and that no special justification is necessary if a law merely has the effect of prohibiting religious exercise. Many would argue that this is a departure from the standard of "compelling" government interest before even a neutral, generally applicable law or regulation could penalize religious practice. This is an important debate.

Employment Division vs Smith raises a second important issue: the religious liberty rights of indigenous people. The denial of constitutional protection for the use of the traditional peyote sacrament touches at the core of the religious freedom of native Americans. The same issue was raised by a 1988 Supreme Court judgment which upheld the right of the US Forest Service to build a logging road through a mountaintop area held sacred by three tribes, even though (as the Court said) the road would "virtually destroy the Indians' ability to practise their religion".

Not long after he arrived in the "New World", Christopher Columbus wrote to the Spanish court that native inhabitants "would easily be made Christians, because it seemed to me that they had no religion". This misperception about indigenous people, who have a deep spirituality and rich religious heritage, has undergirded policies of conquest, colonization and conversion in many parts of the world in the past five hundred years.

It is important to recognize the significance of the religions of indigenous people and to ensure full religious liberty for them. As a UN study concluded:

> The concept of religion must include not only what have been considered the "world's great religions" but also other beliefs or creeds which essentially fulfill the same functions. Within this wider view of religious rights and practices, recognition and protection must be given to all forms of religion which seek the moral improvement of human beings and foster understanding and brotherly love among them... Despite intensive campaigns of proselytization and catechization over a number of centuries, the indigenous people have to a large extent retained their own religions or religious beliefs, sometimes in combination with other creeds.[10]

Church-state tensions have often arisen in authoritarian societies when Christians have actively expressed their faith by taking part in struggles for justice and human rights, out of a conviction that social and political manifestation of belief is an integral part of religious liberty. In the absence of organized political groups, churches may assume or have thrust upon them roles which make them special targets of governments. In many situations, the church has become or provided the only space for dissent and defence of human rights. In defending human rights for all, the church sees itself as making use of and promoting religious liberty, while in the eyes of the state it is seen as overstepping its legitimate bounds.

Actions motivated by religion might well claim some privilege, though this is limited by the fact that any action can claim religious motivation. In the US, Wogaman notes, "courts have held that religious motivation for actions creates a privilege unless the state can show that a compelling state interest cannot be accommodated without restricting such religiously motivated action".[11] It is usually possible for the state to make such a showing. But the requirement at least grants a certain presumption in favour of religious motivation and thereby pays tribute to the importance of such motivation.

But there is another side to this question. Theo van Boven has raised the issue of religious motivation in connection with the sanctuary movement, in which churches have provided refuge to asylum-seekers threatened by deportation. Would it be fair, he asks, "if those who on the basis of their religious convictions provide sanctuary or a safe place to refugees or to illegal immigrants would be put in a more advantageous position than others who would do the same work but who would not claim religious motivations? Are the latter not entitled to the same rights we are claiming for the sanctuary movement on the basis of religious liberty? Or, to put it differently, should the sanctuary movement make its claims on the principles of justice and human rights or on the basis of the legitimate exercise of the freedom of religions?"[12]

Even where constitutional provisions and legislative enactments affirm the principle of religious liberty, such freedom is not necessarily ensured in practice. There are unfortunately many instances of persecution or other manifestations of religious intolerance even where the laws provide religious freedom.

Discrimination on the basis of religion or abridgment of religious liberty may take place in several ways. The special status given by a constitution to one "official" or state religion can in effect mean discriminatory practices against other religions. Sometimes a particular ideology is given a special status. The constitutions of several former socialist states included the right to disseminate anti-religious propaganda while denying the right to disseminate religious propaganda. Sometimes one or several religions are recognized by legislation to the detriment of other religious denominations or beliefs. In some countries the law lists recognized denominations and places them under state control. In some cases the constitution specifies the religious minorities to which legal status is granted and excludes other religious minorities. Discrimination is carried to the extreme when the law declares religions or denominations to be unlawful and punishes the act of belonging to or practising them. There are constitutions and laws which prohibit proselytism and regard conversion or apostasy as a punishable crime.

In addition to or even in the absence of restrictive legislation, governments may employ administrative measures and institute policies which result in discrimination and intolerance against religions. Some governments intervene in internal matters of religious organizations. Media controlled by or approved by the government may seek to denounce, denigrate or ridicule religious values or slander the spiritual leaders of a particular religious community. Some use the school system and textbooks to promote particular religious ideas or to criticize some religions.

The replies given by the governments to the Special Rapporteur of the UN Human Rights Commission which we cited in chapter 2 are revealing. Justification is sought for governments' action against particular religions or what their followers would call religious activities in the name of "national unity", "traditional values of the people", "civic duties" and "national security" — all in addition to terms like "public morality" and "public order", which as we have seen find a place in many constitutions.

Perhaps the most direct way in which many governments try to monitor activities of religious organizations is through legislative enactments on registration. Recognition is accorded only to organizations which are registered, and the government sets conditions for eligibility for registration. At least one government has claimed the sovereign right to grant or refuse authorization. Some governments have gone to the extent of deciding whether an organization or group is a religion or not. Religious liberty is denied to the Baha'is in Iran because Baha'ism is considered by Islam as heresy and therefore is not recognized as a religion by the Iranian government.

One religious group which has met with formidable difficulties and severe and frequent persecution in many countries is the Jehovah's Witnesses. Not only dictatorships of all varieties but also democracies have adopted repressive measures against them and persecuted them. They are banned by several governments to this day. On the basis of their precepts and teachings on state and government, Jehovah's Witnesses do not participate in any political activity, do not vote and do not hold any public office. They refuse to salute national flags or sing national anthems. Many governments, interpreting such activities as anti-national, regard Jehovah's Witnesses as unpatriotic enemies of the secular state. Some governments do not consider Jehovah's Witnesses as a religion at all. As we saw in chapter 2, the group is banned in Indonesia since, according to the government, "its teachings are contrary to the true Christian faith". The government of Indonesia thus takes upon itself not only the right to judge what is true Christian faith but also to ban something which is contrary to the Christian faith and still claims to be Christian.

In the mid-1970s the WCC took up with the government of Malawi the issue of religious liberty of Jehovah's Witnesses there. Jehovah's Witnesses returning from Mozambique were persecuted — some were reportedly tortured and killed by members of the youth wing of the ruling party — because they refused to accept membership in the party, which all Malawi citizens were compelled to do. The World Council of Churches appealed on 31 May 1976 to the president of Malawi to stop the persecution of Jehovah's Witnesses. After the president learned about the appeal (not through the letter sent, but through a BBC broadcast about it) the policy reportedly changed for the better, at least for the time being.

Governments often allege "foreign influence" and "foreign connections" in the activities of some religious organizations and consider collaboration with foreigners in religious activities a threat to national interests. Members of some religious communities are equated with "foreign agents" and, depending on the particular case, regarded as "spies" or agents of "colonialism", "imperialism" or "Zionism". Many governments have strict laws regarding "missionary activities". Some countries which allow their nationals the right to propagate religion deny that right to foreigners.

The right to cross international frontiers for religious purposes and the right to form a free religious association in one's own country are two vital elements of religious freedom. Such freedoms are linked to the universality of religions. Free movement from country to country can be important for the development of religious groups within countries and may be seen as the international face of the freedom of association.

It has become common for governments to justify their policies with regard to religions in the name of the elastic concept of "national interest". National interests are what a particular regime in power perceives to be the interests of the nation, and often can scarcely be distinguished from the interests of the particular regime or the ruling party. Governments sometimes find it expedient to coopt the religious groups in their domestic and international policies.

This is nothing new. As James E. Wood points out:

> The compromise of religion to serve political ends may be coerced as the price to be paid for social acceptance or for obtaining certain favours from the state. The accommodation may also be the result of the manipulation of religion to aid in the accomplishment of national goals and priorities, to which any national church is particularly vulnerable. In any case, the consequence is the subordination of religion to self-interests of the state, an all too familiar phenomenon in the history of religion.[13]

Demands to conform to and support "natural interests" are especially intense at the time of emergencies like war. When the issue of loyalty is raised, it demands great courage on the part of the churches to challenge the government. The governments often seek such a declaration of loyalty because of the influence churches are seen to have on public opinion. Or they hope that church support will legitimize or even sanctify government policies and actions. It is interesting to note that political leaders use moral categories and religious terminology to justify their actions in the name of "national interests".

As Wood points out, "for the churches to dissent from what the nation's leaders declare to be the 'national interests' is for the churches to risk political disfavour, even reprisals, and to have their right to speak out on public affairs challenged as inappropriate and even unpatriotic'".[14] When the church becomes a follower of the state in the name of "national interests", it fails to be the church and thereby surrenders its real mission to the world.

NOTES

[1] H.G. Wood, *Religious Liberty Today*, Cambridge, Cambridge University Press, 1949, pp.2-3.
[2] M. Searle Bates, *Religious Liberty, an Enquiry*, New York/London, International Missionary Council, 1945, p.321.
[3] Philip Wogaman, *Christian Perspectives on Politics*, London, SCM, 1988, p.188.
[4] Elizabeth Odio Benito, *Study on the Current Dimensions of the Problems of Intolerance and Discrimination on Grounds of Religion or Belief*, United Nations, Commission on Human Rights, 1986.
[5] William R. Estep, *The Anabaptist Story*, Nashville, TN, Bradman Press, 1975, pp.194-195.
[6] *Journal of Law and Religion*, vol. 8, no. 5, 1990, p.9.
[7] Robert T. Miller, "Religious Conscience in Colonial New England", in *Readings on Church and State*, ed. James E. Wood Jr, Waco, TX, J.M. Dawson Institute of Church-State Studies, 1989, p.10 and 21.
[8] A.F. Carillo de Albornoz, *The Basis of Religious Liberty*, London, SCM, 1963, pp.136-137.
[9] "Religious Freedom", *Beijing Review*, 4-19 November 1991, p.30.
[10] José R. Martinez Cobo, *Study of the Problem of Discrimination Against Indigenous Populations*, New York/Geneva, United Nations, 1982, p.21.
[11] Wogaman, *op. cit.*, p.199.
[12] Theo van Boven "Religious Witness and Practice in Political and Social Life as an Element of Religious Liberty", in *Religious Liberty: CCIA Background Information*, 1987, no. 1, p.20.
[13] James E. Wood Jr, "Religion and National Interests", in *Journal of Church and State*, vol. 32, no. 1, 1990, p.15.
[14] *Ibid.*

5. Religions and Religious Liberty

Progress towards religious liberty is mainly due to the work of civil authorities and intergovernmental organizations rather than to religious bodies. Historically, recognition of religious liberty has not been a characteristic of religion as such.

Indeed, Wood notes, "resistance to religious liberty is deeply rooted in the history of religion, in which coercion, intolerance and persecution have played a major role". Denial of the right of dissent has been the norm: "Violations of the sense of the sacred or denials of religious truth were not to be tolerated." He attributes the concept of religious liberty to "the demythologizing of political authority, the emergence of the modern nation state, the decline of religious authority in political affairs, the development of treaties between nations with differing religious traditions, the growth of religious pluralism within nations, and the advances towards constitutional and democratic governments".[1]

The subject of this chapter is one which churches should examine with a high degree of self-criticism and a sense of humility. With a few notable exceptions, neither in theory nor in practice has the Hebrew-Christian tradition promoted religious liberty but has often violated it. In fact the monotheistic prophetic type of religion that has long been dominant in the Middle East and the West has been generally detrimental to the exercise of the most important kinds of freedom.

It may appear paradoxical that intolerance is so deeply ingrained in a religion based on freedom in Christ. In Hans Küng's words, "the Christian's freedom, with its paradoxical harmonization of independence and duties, power and renunciation, autonomy and service, dominion and slavery is a mystery to the world".[2]

Yet Guido de Ruggiero has written that "the antagonist in the struggle of mankind for religious freedom has been Christianity, which accentuated the elements of intolerance included in the Hebraic heritage and supplemented them by the introduction of two new and potent incentives, the idea of a universal mission and a rigid dogma, the conception of the church as an indispensable mediator between God and man".[3]

The universal monotheism of the Hebrew-Christian tradition seems automatically to define those who do not accept or worship God as being in error (at best) or possibly even as being the enemies of God. The result was religious exclusivism and the branding of other faiths as fallen and in error. The Hebrew God was a jealous God to be worshipped and obeyed under the penalty of death.

Passages from the Old Testament can be quoted in support of intolerance of the worst kind:

> One who blasphemes the name of the Lord shall be put to death; the whole congregation shall stone the blasphemer. Aliens as well as citizens, when they blaspheme the Name, shall be put to death (Lev. 24:16).
>
> If anyone secretly entices you — even if it is your brother... or your own son or daughter, or the wife you embrace, or your most intimate friend — saying, "let us go worship other gods"... you must not yield to or heed any such persons. Show them no pity or compassion and do not shield them. But you shall surely kill them; your own hand shall be first against them to execute them, and afterwards the hand of all the people (Deut. 13:6-9).

Wogaman points out that these passages by no means come from "an early, more primitive stage in the development of Hebrew religion". Deuteronomy was probably written after the time of the great eighth-century prophets Amos, Hosea, Isaiah and Micah; and Leviticus is evidently even later.[4]

The exclusive nature of the monotheistic religions and the consequent intolerance towards and repression of those outside have been evident in the development of Judaism, Christianity and Islam. In marked contrast is the heritage of some of the Asian religions. Twenty-three centuries ago King Ashoka, patron of Buddhism, recommended to his subjects that they should act in accordance with a principle of toleration.

> Acting thus, we contribute to our creed by serving others. Acting otherwise, we harm our own faith, bringing discredit upon the others. He who exalts his own belief, discrediting all others, does so surely to obey his religion with the intention of making a display of it. But behaving thus, he gives it the hardest blows. And for this reason concord is good only in so far as all listen to each other's creeds and live to listen to them.

Reflected here is the well-known Buddhist tradition of tolerance, which can be traced back to Hinduism, in which tolerance was the result of understanding religion as a path to God. There can be different paths to God, and it is religious life that is important, not the dogma. The mystical and syncretic elements of Hinduism promoted tolerance and played a significant role in the religious history of Asia. Newman points out that nothing in Oriental history compares "in magnitude, severity, organization or duration to the systematic restriction of religious liberty that marks so much of European history. This cultural difference is largely to be explained on the basis of divergent religious conceptions and divergent conceptions of religion."[5]

Islam prescribes severe penalties for those who change from the Islamic faith, considering this not only a violation of the compact of submission made with God, but also a breach of contract with God's representatives on earth. Thus it constitutes apostasy and treason punishable by death. While Islam shows a degree of toleration for non-Muslim monotheists (Jews and Christians), they are hardly accorded full and equal rights. Yet so long as they live peaceably, they may practise their religion.

Some of the attitude of intolerance in the Old Testament is carried on into the New Testament, despite the emphasis on freedom. Influenced by Hellenistic philosophy, Paul was largely responsible for laying the foundation of subsequent Christian reflection on the nature of freedom. But elsewhere in the New Testament one finds such sharp and intolerant expressions of exclusivism as these:

> Everyone who does not abide in the teaching of Christ but goes beyond it, does not have God; whoever abides in this teaching has both the Father and the Son. Do not receive into the house or welcome anyone who comes to you and does not bring this teaching; for to welcome is to participate in the evil deeds of such a person (2 John 9-11).
>
> There will be false teachers among you, who will secretly bring in destructive opinions. They will even deny the Master who bought them — bringing swift destruction on themselves (2 Pet. 2:1).

To be sure, these passages were written at a time when there was an agonizing debate going on in the church about doctrine.

Wogaman points out that monotheism can also be understood — and indeed has been understood in biblical and post-biblical history — in a way that is congenial to religious liberty:

That is the notion that since God transcends any man, culture or society, it ill behooves any man to make pretentious claims on the basis of which intolerance and persecution might be grounded. If God is sovereign Lord of all, no man can justly claim to know all about God's intentions at every time and place in human history. No man can have unlimited confidence that God, the sovereign Lord of all the ages, has spoken only to him or to his community.[6]

There is ample biblical evidence of the prophetic critique of both the nationalistic and religious pretensions of the Israelites, as well as expressions of concern for the welfare of other nations and peoples. Even the book of Leviticus, from which we earlier cited a passage reflecting intolerance, includes this straightforward appeal for tolerance to strangers:

When an alien resides with you in your land, you shall not oppress the alien. The alien who resides with you shall be to you as the citizen among you; you shall love the alien as yourself, for you were aliens in the land of Egypt: I am the Lord your God (Lev. 19:33).

It should be remembered that in the first three centuries the question was not whether Christianity would be tolerant but whether Christianity would survive at all in the hostile climate of a Roman empire largely devoted to other faiths — including worship of the emperor. Then things changed radically. Constantine's edict of 313 provided for individual freedom of conscience, for full rights to Christianity on equality with other recognized religions and for the restoration of church property which had been confiscated. Favour led to privilege, which turned to prestige; and the church soon became very powerful.

Then the church and the state turned on the heretics. The codes of Theodosius and Justinian forbade heretics to build churches, to assemble for religious purposes or to teach their doctrines even in private. They were denied rights of bequest, inheritance, even of contract. Death was prescribed for those who lapsed from Christianity into pagan rites. Bates points out that some of these measures in the codes of Theodosius and Justinian appealed to medieval and early modern states on into the Reformation. "In their religious bearings they entered into common law and have formed the basis of the Catholic state."

> Already men were at work to support from the scriptures the measures of compulsion and punishment which they desired to inflict by state authority or other means. The Old Testament was then and thereafter to be searched for passages prescribing death penalties for idolatry, blasphemy and apostasy which could be inflicted upon heresy as well. The New Testament provided little in material penalties but was richer in the content and destructive support of strict orthodoxy. From the two Testaments taken together, the dogmatist, the bigot, the man of faction, the literalist, the bureaucrat, the sadist have been able to justify their will, that day until now.[7]

Yet there were also significant Christian voices down the centuries upholding religious liberty. Justin Martyr wrote at the end of the second century that "nothing is more contrary to religion than restraint". Tertullian was even more emphatic: "It is a fundamental human right, a privilege of nature, that every man should worship according to his own convictions... It is not in the nature of religion to coerce religion, which must be adopted freely and not by force." The position taken by Lactantius was even more principled: "It is only in religion that liberty has chosen to dwell. For nothing is so much a matter of free will as religion, and no one can be required to worship what he does not will to worship."

But it was not these voices who determined the policies of either church or state. A.J. Carlyle describes the church of the middle ages as "intolerant, the source and author of persecution", defending "the most violent measures which could be taken against those who differed from it... The church ceased to be the protector of the spiritual liberty of the individual and... became its most formidable enemy."[8]

The popes took an unequivocal position. Gregory VII late in the eleventh century declared that "the pontiff alone is able to bind and to loose, to give and take away, according to the merits of each man". Boniface VII said that every human being, as a necessary condition of salvation, "should be subject to the Roman pope".

The most influential theologians spoke in equally strong terms. St Augustine declared heresy worse than murder, because it destroys the soul rather than the body. Thomas Aquinas called the counterfeiting of God's truth worse than the forging of the prince's coins — for which death was the accepted penalty — and said heresy separates man from God more than all other sins and thus is to be punished more severely. No wonder that the Inquisition was instituted.

In a perceptive essay Charles E. Curran points out that Western Christianity has taken a long time and a tortuous path to arrive at its acceptance of religious liberty and fundamental rights. "In general, Roman Catholic and mainline Protestant Christianity contributed little or nothing to the original acceptance of religious liberty in the West. Church and theological support for religious liberty in the West came only after religious liberty had been well accepted in the world at large. Protestantism in general embraced religious liberty much earlier than Roman Catholicism."[9]

The separation of church and state and the breakdown of the old model of Christendom compelled churches to think about their own rights and those of others. With the Reformation, the proliferation of confessions and denominations also pushed in the direction of accepting religious freedom. In coming to this position it was possible for the Roman Catholics and the Protestants to find theological resources. But the process was generally slow and took even longer for Roman Catholics than Protestants.

Curran contends that "the fact that Protestantism embraced religious freedom before Catholicism is not due only to more pragmatic reasons, for in general Protestantism has given more importance to freedom than has Catholicism".[10] After all, Protestantism was a reaction to the authoritarian structure of the church of Rome. Its theology, ethics, political ethics and ecclesiology give a central role to freedom. By contrast, the emphasis in Catholic moral theology tended to fall on order.

But for centuries the particular forms church-state relations took in predominantly Catholic and Protestant countries and the privileges the churches enjoyed limited their capacity to build on their own theological resources for advocating human rights in general and religious freedom in particular. Over several centuries whatever power and influence the church acquired was misused, leading not only to intolerance but to active persecution of those who dissented.

James Wood's graphic summary of several thousand years of religious intolerance may serve as a sobering reminder of why it is important for churches today actively to promote dialogue among religions and creatively to seek ways of strengthening pluralist societies by promoting religious freedom for all:

> Examples of religious persecution have clearly not been restricted to any one era or to any one religion: the conflict over Ikhnaton's monotheism in Egypt, the suppression of the Canaanites by the Israelites, the execution of Socrates, the crucifixion of Jesus, the martyrdom of Christians by the Roman emperors, the condemnation of heretics and schismatics by the Christian church, the intolerance of Muslim invaders, the crusades of Christians against Muslims, the repeated persecutions and the pogroms against Jews by Christians, the persecution of Protestants by Catholics, the persecution of Catholics by Protestants, the Catholic and Protestant attacks on Anabaptists and other free churches, the persecution of "witches" and Quakers in early Massachusetts, the persecution of Baptists in New England and Virginia, the persecution of Catholics throughout colonial America, and, in more recent decades, the repeated harassment of non-conventional faiths such as the Jehovah's Witnesses, the Worldwide Church of God, the Church of Scientology, and the Unification Church.[11]

NOTES

[1] James E. Wood Jr, "Religions and Religious Liberty", *Journal of Church and State*, vol. 33, no. 2, 1991, p.225.
[2] Hans Küng, *The Church*, London, Burnes & Oates Ltd, 1967, p.156.
[3] Guido de Ruggiero, *Encyclopedia of the Social Sciences*, vol. XIII, p.241, quoted in M. Searle Bates, *Religious Liberty, an Inquiry*, New York/London, International Missionary Council, 1945, p.132.
[4] Philip Wogaman, *Protestant Faith and Religious Liberty*, Nashville, TN, Abingdon, 1967, p.91.
[5] Jay Newman, *On Religious Freedom*, Toronto, University of Toronto Press, 1991, p.102.
[6] Wogaman, *op. cit.*, p.94.
[7] M. Searle Bates, *Religious Liberty, an Enquiry*, *op. cit.*, p.135.
[8] A.J. Carlyle, *The Christian Church and Liberty*, London, J. Clarke, 1924, p.96.
[9] Charles E. Curran, "Religious Freedom — Human Rights in the World and the Church", in *Religious Liberty and Human Rights*, ed. L. Swidler, Philadelphia, Ecumenical Press, 1986, p.145.
[10] *Ibid.*, p.146.
[11] Wood, *op. cit.*

6. Some New Developments

The discussion of religious liberty has assumed a new sense of urgency in recent years as religion has re-emerged as a major force on the global scene. In the political developments of a number of countries religion plays a major role. It has become the rallying point and motive force in many nationalist struggles, especially where ethnicity and religion are coterminous. Elsewhere, religious convictions have given stimulus and direction to the democratic transformation of societies and the defence and promotion of human rights. In the dramatic decline of communism and the break-up of socialist societies, religion played an important transitional role and is now faced with new avenues, new possibilities of growth and influence.

These trends and developments do not necessarily form a single phenomenon; they are a mixture of varying and even contradictory forces. But they all have implications for religious liberty, since they redefine relations between religion and the state and among religious communities.

In the 1950s and 1960s it was fashionable to speak about the secularization and the decline — even the possible disappearance — of religion. It was argued that modernization would weaken or even destroy religion's grip over traditional cultures, reduce the political significance of religion and diminish individual attachment to religious values. At best, it was thought, it would remain the private affair of the individual, but it would lose its force for collective action, social control and political mobilization.

It is now apparent that this was basically a Western approach, based on the Western experience of separation between religion and politics. The claims that industrialization and urbanization would weaken traditional institutions like religion and lead to the depoliticization of religion became part of the development package offered to the newly independent countries of Asia, Africa and Latin America. Secularization, which was often presented as secularism, came along with modernization and Westernization. The deep and continuing influence of religion in many of these countries was vastly underestimated.

Western theologians joined with sociologists in propounding theories about the decline of institutional religion.

Harvey Cox eloquently describes what has happened to these theories:

> In 1965, much under the influence of Bonhoeffer's theology and greatly concerned about what the expected decline of traditional religion might do to the relevance of Christianity, I wrote a book called *The Secular City*. The world of declining religion to which my earlier book was addressed has begun to change in ways that few people anticipated. A new age that some call the "postmodern" has begun to appear. Rather than an era of rampant secularization and religious decline, it appears to be more of an era of religious revival and the return of the sacred.[1]

The resurgence of religions in many parts of the world has undermined many widely held ideas about modernization. Religious values, sentiments and structures today are being used to create forces for social change; and Anson Shupe says that "it will not do to try to dismiss the religious factor as an epiphenomenon or as some simple last-gasp backlash against social change".[2]

The struggle between religion and politics is age-old. Both are about power, though not necessarily the same kind of power. But their roles as they deal with human affairs have always been overlapping. Both often vie for the same territory. This contest varies in nature and intensity from time to time and from country to country. Both religion and politics can make absolutist claims. Both can be totalitarian. Advances in technology and in the sophistication of the techniques of coercion in the modern period have enabled politics, with its instrument the state, to claim more territory. But there has been a backlash.

In early history religion's influence and power were all-embracing, and it was not possible to distinguish between the religious and political realms. As Huston Smith writes: "Without the mandate of heaven, the Chinese emperors were no more than commoners, while Islam's most effective political years were those in which the Caliphate, an office in which sacred and secular were combined, was a reality. In Europe, once the doctrine of the divine right of kings was abandoned, kingship was no longer taken seriously... At their start, the great historical religions looked more like civilizations than like religions as currently conceived; they were prescriptions for ordering the entire range of human affairs, economics, politics, ethics, law, philosophy, art and diet."[3]

As the modern state evolved during the course of history, it took over much of this prescriptive role. Secularization pushed religion to the individual's private life and to the fringes of society. Of course the terms "secularization" and "secularism" are often used loosely and imprecisely. German theologian Dietrich Bonhoeffer described secularization as "a movement towards the autonomy of man, in which I would include the discovery of the laws by which the world lives and deals with itself in science, social and political matters, art, ethics and religion".[4] Secularism, in spite of the negative connotations it had for religion, was considered the best policy for a state to guarantee religious freedom without favouring any particular religion or confession.

In India, secularism has constitutional sanctity and is generally understood to mean religious neutrality. At least three factors shaped Indian secularism. One was the scientific humanism of Jawaharlal Nehru, who said the new industrial plants would be the new temples of India. A second was Gandhi's respect for all religions, which grew out of the traditional Hindu understanding of religion. The third was the Congress Party's political platform of secularism, as opposed to the theocratic platform of the Muslim League, which wanted to establish an Islamic state. The concept of secularism is now under challenge from Hindu fundamentalists.

Shupe has argued that the globalization of secularization soon found its limits. This globalization led to a clash of cultures and challenged the truth claims of various traditional religions. At some point, he says, "globalization sets in motion the dynamic for a search for ultimate meaning, values and resacralization. In other words, secularization turns in on itself and generates the very conditions for a resurgence of religious influence (albeit perhaps an innovative or unconventional religion)."[5]

The new situation was described in a 1981 WCC study document as follows:

> In many parts of the third world, there is taking place a religious renaissance with a strong socio-political component

which challenges the modernist and secularist ideologies of the North, both East and West. The fact is that a large number of communities consider religion as an important focus both in the struggle for liberation from oppression and the struggle for critical self-identity and development, in terms of their own historical ethos. In an increasing number of "periphery" countries, such perceptions have begun to conflict with "modernization" models as propagated or imposed by "centre" countries, since these models are seen not as promoting true development, but on the contrary, as distorting development and perpetuating underdevelopment. And since such misdevelopment has been associated with secularization, disenchantment with the former has gone hand in hand with disenchantment with the latter. And because Christian theology has been able to accept and even legitimize this secular development, Christianity itself tends increasingly to become a target, along with secularism, of religious reaction.[6]

The paper went on to observe that this reaction gave legitimacy to a variety of fundamentalist movements, Christian and otherwise. "In every fundamentalism there is an element of return to purity, to the source from which to retrieve the power of revival. As such, fundamentalism is a basic kind of affirmation of historic identity and integrity of peoples, in which religion is a formative element. This often brings fundamentalism into a radical opposition to the imposition of ideological, religious and institutional structures emanating from the history of another region of the world."[7]

Hassan-al-Turabi, the architect of Islamic-based laws (sharia) in Sudan in 1983, one of the most articulate proponents of Islamic fundamentalism, describes its march as inevitable as it moves to fill the vacuum left by the failure of Western-inspired African socialism and Arab nationalism. "Islam is the only force that remains in this part of the world. There is nothing else left to inspire the young, to mobilize them, to give them a vision, a sense of allegiance."[8]

The contemporary resurgence of religion is explained by some sociologists as a response to a multi-faceted crisis in the twentieth century, stemming, Sahliyeh says:

> from the inconclusive modernizing efforts of secular elites in the third world, growing disillusionment with secular nationalism, problems of legitimacy and political oppression in many developing countries, problems of national identity, widespread socio-

economic grievances, and the erosion of the traditional morality and values both in the West and the third world... Religion provides the aggrieved with a sense of refuge, guidance, comfort and a sense of discipline to cope with the complexities of life.[9]

In many countries secularist development models neither provided the economic emancipation they promised nor did they strengthen the political processes. They often benefited the elites, but the vast majority of the population was left out. Significantly, the criticism of these economic and political models was often articulated by Western-educated elites. To quote Sahliyeh, "the political utilization of religion can therefore be seen as part of the third world's quest for political, economic and cultural autonomy and authenticity".[10]

But there were also instances in which regimes that had lost their support tried to legitimize them by using religion. Sudan is a case in point.

I visited Sudan in early 1978 along with Leopoldo Niilus, then director of the WCC's Commission of the Churches on International Affairs. After going to the predominantly Christian south, where we heard concerns about the possible introduction of sharia in Sudan, we met with President Nimeiri. He was categorical in his commitment to a secular Sudan and affirmed that he would never allow the introduction of sharia. The agreement of 1972, which had ended the civil war, and the unity of the country were still the foundation of the support he enjoyed. However, a series of policy errors narrowed and weakened his political base and in 1983, as a last resort for political survival, he introduced sharia by a decree. When I met him again in 1984 he was obviously uncomfortable in his new role as the president of an Islamic state.

The only way to understand Islamic revivalism is through contextual analysis, for, as Edward Said notes, "Islam varies from place to place subject to both history and geography".[11] Nor should revivalism be identified with fundamentalism. A revival does not have to be fundamentalistic. And it is not correct or fair to assume revivalism or fundamentalism means militant violence. The impact of Islamic fundamentalism on politics is a much debated issue.

The basic question is whether it is conceivable for vibrant Islam to exist without Islamic dominion? Muslim fundamentalists say no. Yet experience disputes this claim. Pakistan, founded as a state separate from the rest of India largely because of its Muslim population, has had three constitutions since 1948 and remains uncertain about the feasibility of Islamic law governing all social and economic relations. In Iran, the principle that ultimate judicial and legislative authority resides in the ayatollah as the legitimate successor of Mohammed did not survive Khomeini's death. The contradictions of sharing power between an elected legislative assembly and an unimpeachable clerical establishment led to the abolition of the supreme religious authority in the revised constitution.[12]

Resurgence in other religions has sometimes had political implications as well. Within Christianity this has ranged from fundamentalist Christians rallying support for a conservative stance on national and international political issues to liberation theologies inspiring political action for justice and human dignity by the marginalized. The church has sometimes been thrust into a position of political opposition, especially in situations in which all opposition movements and groups have been banned and the church has become the only space for dissent and defence of human rights. In many places in the developing world, religion has become the only vehicle for the articulation of popular grievances.

A variety of factors facilitate this: charismatic religious leadership, developed organizational structures, communication networks, physical facilities (churches, mosques, etc.). Sacred texts from the Bible or the Quran have proved to be more powerful than United Nations declarations and national constitutions both as motives and as basis for political action.

Some analysts caution against generalizing about or over-emphasizing religious resurgence. "Liberation theologians and revolutionary ayatollahs may be aware of each other's existence," Donald Smith has observed, "but have not influenced each other very much."[13] They point out that religious resurgence is a recurring, cyclical phenomenon. Yet even if sweeping claims about a global religious renaissance and a simultaneous reversal of secularism may not be upheld, the role of religion in public life, its relevance to modern society and its capacity to adapt to the requirements of modernization must be acknowledged. "Traditional religions are not simply fading away," Sahliyeh concludes. "Their political role seems to be a lasting feature in many contemporary political systems."[14]

The implications of religious resurgence for human rights in general and religious liberty in particular are often adverse. It may challenge pluralism and make religions unequal in their social rights. Adherents of religions other than the dominant one may find themselves in a second-class status in society at large and even within the legal system on the basis of the exclusivist claims and the direct and indirect influence of a religion on the state. Leaders of the dominant religion in some instances have claimed that whenever a conflict arises, the prescriptions of that religion take precedence over internationally recognized human rights. As Theo van Boven observes, "this position defies squarely the concept of universality of human rights which underlies the whole movement for the promotion and protection of human rights as embodied in the United Nations Charter, the Universal Declaration of Human Rights and subsequent international instruments in the field of human rights".[15]

Pointing out the challenge from revivalism, Gabriel Habib has emphasized the need for a spirit of self-criticism on the part of the church. He said revivalism is "challenging the very basis of pluralism and secular society as we have lived them within the framework of the modern nation-state. However, when we approach this subject, we should do so with humility..., with a sense of repentance and self-criticism."[16]

Religion plays a significant role in many ethnic and nationalist conflicts. If these conflicts become violent, religious motivations may add to the militancy. The roles religion plays in conflicts were identified in a 1985 WCC report as follows:
— religion is a component of nationalism;
— religious factors exacerbate tensions or conflicts whose root causes are socio-political and economic;
— religious factors and sentiments are deliberately used to heighten tensions;
— religious notions of the state transform political institutions, leading to conflicts;
— religious fundamentalism influences state policies substantially;

— growing lack of confidence by minorities or other underprivileged groups leads to opposition and conflictual use of religion;
— religious conflicts are used by outside forces to destabilize countries.

Each of these has implications for religious liberty.

Especially — though not exclusively — in the West, the rise and growth of New Religious Movements has raised new problems in religious liberty and church-state relations. Behind the emergence of New Religious Movements are many of the same factors that have contributed to religious renaissance, but in their innovation, creativity, ways of functioning and challenges to customarily accepted norms of religion, the New Religious Movements are distinct. In particular, they seem to challenge mainline religions and thus meet resistance and hostility from several quarters.

Mainline religious bodies, state authorities and society as a whole hesitate to recognize these movements as authentic religions, referring to them as "cults", a term obviously used in a prejudicial and even derogatory manner. A strong "anti-cult" movement has arisen in Europe and North America where many of the new religions have made significant inroads. In fact, many religions were at one time or other called cults, including Quakers, Mennonites and Methodists. History shows that many of the movements which are at first called cults gradually gain social acceptance and even influence.

A WCC-Lutheran World Federation consultation in Amsterdam in 1986 noted that

> the term "New Religious Movements" covers a vast range of movements that are very different from one another in their origins and belief, their structure and organization and their self-understanding... There are movements which have their origins in the Eastern traditions; there are those that have arisen more as sectarian movements with origins in the Christian tradition; there are those that have arisen in the encounter of primal traditions or tribal societies with universal religions; and there is also a range of occult and gnostic groups... We must be careful that our response to a particular movement or its particular excesses does not colour our understanding of New Religious Movements as a whole.[17]

Part of the appeal of new religions lies in the declining influence of conventional religious organizations and their failure to meet people's spiritual needs. This is often linked to material success and the spiritual vacuum it reinforces. A Vatican study says New Religious Movements appear to respond to the quest for belonging or a sense of community, the search for answers, the search for wholeness, the search for cultural identity, the need to be recognized, to be special, the search for transcendence, the need for spiritual guidance, the need for vision, the need for participation and involvement.[18]

Often these groups meet not only intolerance and hostility but also denial of fundamental freedoms. A number of reasons can be suggested for the "anti-cult" attitude and consequent infringement of religious liberty. One is the hostility evoked by extremist movements, of which the most often-cited case is the mass suicide-murder of more than 900 adults and children connected with the People's Temple of Jim Jones in Jonestown, Guyana, more than a decade ago. Another is the general perception of these movements as a threat to conventional religious groups, accelerating the leakage of members from them. However, because of the non-traditional way in which New Religious Movements function, they are generally perceived as a threat to the social order.

Perhaps the greatest controversy about the New Religious Movements centres on their method of conversion. Frequently it is alleged that they use psychological and even physical coercion to recruit converts and keep them under discipline. There have been persistent charges of the use of techniques of "mind control" and brainwashing to enslave converts, break up families and imprison members. In a number of US court cases, huge monetary judgments have been awarded against such groups as the Church of Scientology, Hare Krishna Movement and Unification Church.

As James E. Wood says: "While the unpopularity of any non-conventional religion may be explainable and even understandable, there can be no justification for the denial of its (or of one of its adherents') constitutional right to the free exercise of religion and its right to religious equality under the law so long as that religion operates in compliance with civil and criminal law as applied to all other religions".[19]

Some church leaders have been vocal in attacking New Religious Movements, but in the US the major religious bodies have not joined such attacks. Many feel that the prospect of governmental intervention against the New Religious Movements would pose a threat to the free exercise of religion and church autonomy in general.

Dean M. Kelley points out that attacks on the activities of New Religious Movements have often invoked laws which were not originally intended for such application. "Legal prosecutions have been instituted, not because of excessive zeal on the part of public officials, but as a result of complaints and goadings by irate citizens." Kelley describes the main lines of attack as follows: denying or revoking tax exemptions, regulating or restricting solicitations of charitable contributions, rigorous prosecution of New Religious Movement leaders for violations ignored by the authorities in most other cases.[20]

The WCC-LWF consultation stated that in the realm of human rights and religious liberty — the right of New Religious Movements to exist and to gain adherents by conversion —

> further distinctions could be made: persons should be free to speak their religious convictions virtually without exception. In the realm of action, however, claims of religious liberty should not normally provide a defence for the violation of criminal law, such as the perpetration of violence upon others, but exceptions to civil law on the basis of religious commitment should be permitted by governments, even if modifications of law may be necessary, unless such actions can be shown to be harmful to others.[21]

The report warns that "religious liberty cannot be claimed by some if it is denied to others"[22] and recalls the long and shameful history of both religious and civil persecution of New Religious Movements. It should not be forgotten that the early story of the struggle for religious liberty is of sects establishing an identity of their own with their members being freed from the obligation of supporting a faith they did not hold.

The collapse of communist governments in the Soviet Union and Central and Eastern Europe has opened up new possibilities for greater religious freedom there. Moreover, the democratic upsurge that preceded these changes and was strengthened by them has a global impact contributing to expansion of human rights. The ideological stance of Marxism had put severe limitations on religious liberty.

The question may be raised whether atheism is a substantial and integral part of Marxism or an accidental or historically conditioned element of it. The atheism of Marx himself was clearly a reaction to the prevailing attitude of the Christian churches of his time. All too frequently, the actual life and activity of the churches confirmed communists in their conviction that religious belief is detrimental to the building of a new society in which human beings find justice and freedom. With Marxism there is an expression of the Old Testament prophetic demand for social justice, for true brotherhood and an end to every form of exploitation and oppression.

Atheism was not the main point in the socialist movement which arose in the second half of the nineteenth century and culminated in the revolution of 1917 and the development of a new social order in Eastern Europe. It would be foolish, nevertheless, not to take this socialist atheism seriously or to regard it as an insignificant aspect of Marxist-Leninist philosophy.

It may be worth looking a bit more closely at the policy of the (former) Soviet Union on religion and religious liberty, since this policy was the model followed in other Eastern European states and influenced policies in a number of Marxist and Marxist-oriented states elsewhere.[23]

The period following the October Revolution in Russia in 1917 was one of direct confrontation between church and state. Church authorities viewed the decree on the separation of church from state and of school from church as not only depriving the church of its privileges but as part of an attempt to destroy the church. Not long thereafter, the approach of the government to religious matters became rather cautious. Greater emphasis was laid on undermining religion by social and economic action rather than by direct confrontation with churches and believers. Lenin himself warned against the danger of offending religious feelings. However, in the early 1920s the Russian Orthodox Church faced considerable difficulties.

At his death in 1924, Lenin left a rather ambiguous legacy concerning religion: "a militantly atheistic outlook tempered by the conviction that the subordination of action against religious bodies to the wider objectives of the state leaves the maximum freedom to pursue whatever policy appears to be the most expedient at any particular juncture", as an observer pointed out.

Certain critical changes in the religious legislation of the Soviet Union were introduced in 1929. A law on religious association was published in April and in October the Instructions of the People's Commissariat of the Interior clarified and supplemented it. These documents, consisting of more than sixty articles telling religious organizations the few things they might do and the many they might not, laid down the rights and duties of individual believers. Revised in 1932, 1962 and again in 1975, this remained the fundamental law on religious matters in the Soviet Union until a new law on freedom of conscience was enacted in the last years of the Union.

From 1929 until 1941 the articles of the law which limited rather than guaranteed religious life and activity were applied with great vigour. This was the period when Stalin's persecution of religious institutions and believers was most intense, and the church suffered acutely. Purges were being carried out at all levels of society in an attempt to eliminate all actual and potential opponents of Stalin. In his meeting with Russian Orthodox Church leaders in April 1988, Mikhail Gorbachev said of this period that "religious organizations were affected by the tragic developments that occurred in the period of the cult of personality. This period was unequivocally assessed as a departure from socialist principles that have now been restored in their rights. Mistakes made with regard to the church and believers in the 1930s and the years that followed are being rectified."

During a visit to the WCC in September 1988, Konstantin Kharchev, chairman of the Council for Religious Affairs, said: "We are ashamed to recall this period. The victims were some of our best people who were totally innocent; but the victims were not only believers, but non-believers and communists too."

Between 1941 and 1959 enforcement of the law was much less rigorous. During the war years, the support of the religious bodies was considered important, and in the desperate circumstances of the time Stalin was keen to maintain the unity of the nation and to mobilize all its resources in defeating the German invaders. There was a tacit "concordat" between church and state, which Stalin used to gain goodwill from Western nations. Surprisingly, this understanding continued for more than a decade after the war.

The situation changed drastically when Nikita Khrushchev came to power. In general he appeared to liberalize policies, but in this period of liberalizing Khrushchev was probably worried that the churches might extend their influence, and he launched an anti-religious campaign in 1959. The party leadership thought that they were close to achieving the goal of communism. In such a period religion had no place. Khrushchev reaffirmed the general direction of the campaign at the 22nd Party Congress: "Now that the building of communism has been broadly undertaken... the Party has put into its programme the task of fully and completely overcoming religious prejudices." Some 10,000 churches were closed during the period. Theological training was severely curtailed. Many bishops, priests, monks and nuns were imprisoned. Some of the extra-legal pressures initiated during this period were subsequently given legal basis.

The campaign against the church ceased in 1964 when Khrushchev was toppled from power. From then on, the law was interpreted and applied more liberally than in the 1930s and in the Khrushchev era. In 1975 it was revised substantially, with amendments for half of the 68 articles.

Article 52 of the Soviet constitution, revised in 1977, stated:

> Freedom of conscience, that is, the right to profess any religion or not to profess any religion, to perform religious rites or to conduct atheist propaganda shall be guaranteed for all citizens of the USSR. Incitement of hostility and hatred on religious grounds shall be prohibited. The church in the USSR shall be separated from the state and the school from the church.

The fundamental law of the state thus maintained an inequality between the believers, who were allowed only to perform religious rites, and atheists, who were allowed to conduct propaganda.

The state organ entrusted with "the aim of consistent realization of the policies of the Soviet state in relation to religion" was the Council for Religious Affairs. It had wide powers and closely monitored the activities of the religious organizations and on various occasions intervened in the affairs of the church.

After the mid-1980s, things began to change rapidly in the wake of *perestroika* and *glasnost*, even without any change in the legislation. Freedom of religion expanded along with other freedoms.

As mentioned earlier, the Soviet Union's policy not only became a model for other socialist states in the region, but also influenced Marxist regimes in the third world. However, there were fundamental differences in policy on religion between the new Marxist states of the 1970s in the third world (they have all given up Marxism) and those of the Soviet Union. In the first years of their experimentation with scientific socialism, the Soviet Union and some of the other socialist states wanted to do away with religion. Most third-world Marxist states wanted to have a viable relationship with the churches, though the methods employed by these third-world regimes to control religious organizations were those applied in the socialist countries.

By the late 1960s Soviet scholarship was beginning to argue that "revolutionary democracies" must avoid confrontational church-state relations and that the disestablishment of organized religion is not a task of the "revolutionary democratic" stage. Rather, Marxist revolutionary states should transform the church into a "people's church", thus making it an instrument of revolution. The disappearance of religion as both an institution and a phenomenon was expected to occur in the stage of "mature" communism.

In the early 1980s when I was a regular visitor to Ethiopia I often met a senior government official, who once told me: "You may ask about religious liberty in Ethiopia. You are a regular visitor here. As you can see, more people go to church now than before the revolution. At this stage we are not worried. We accept this as an objective reality. But it will change as we advance in our revolution." It did not. In January 1990, during the visit of a WCC delegation there, the then-president Mengistu Haile Mariam began his remarks by welcoming the group to the Timkhat festival of the Ethiopian Orthodox Church and telling them of "the great role played by the church in defending Ethiopian nationalism". The Ethiopian government was actively courting the support of the Orthodox church in the civil wars.

As Peter Costea points out: "In deciding on a less radical church policy, the Marxist-Leninist regimes have been guided less by the advice of Soviet scholars and more by matters of realism and pragmatism."[24]

While Marxist states generally maintained that they were secular states practising separation of church and state, control of religious organizations was extensive. Moreover they usually added a limiting provision in legislation on religious liberty. For example, Ethiopia's constitution said: "Ethiopians are guaranteed freedom of conscience and religion. Freedom of religion may not be exercised in a manner contrary to the interest of the state and revolution, public morality and freedom of others." Note the terms "state" and "revolution".

The only state in which religion was banned was Albania. At the outset, the communist government generally followed the Soviet line in its policy on religion, officially guaranteeing believers free practice of religion. In actual fact the guarantees meant very little. The Party used individual terrorism against the clergy and active believers, leading to fake trials, torture and murder. The government undermined and destroyed church institutions.

A 1949 decree confined religious activity to authorized services at specified places of worship. Other decrees followed which all but eliminated any kind of religious freedom. The final stroke came in 1967. By that time Albania was following the Chinese line and extolled the Cultural Revolution initiated by Mao Tse-Tung. The government used youth and party cadres for an intensified struggle against religion and then made all religious practices illegal, though this ban was incorporated into the constitution only in 1976.

Albania vehemently attacked all other communist regimes, including the Soviet Union and, after Mao's death, China, for their "lukewarm, anti-revolutionary" attitude to religion. Albania was the last to fall among the Marxist regimes of Eastern Europe, and it was only very gradually that it began allowing some religious freedom from 1991.

NOTES

[1] Harvey Cox, *Religion in the Secular City*, New York, Simon & Schuster, 1984, pp.19-20.
[2] Anson Shupe, "The Stubborn Persistence of Religion in the Global Arena", in *Religious Resurgence and Politics in the Contemporary World*, ed. Emile Sahliyeh, Albany, State University of New York, 1990, p.18.
[3] Huston Smith, introduction, in *Spirit Matters: The Worldwide Impact of Religion in Contemporary Politics*, ed. Richard L. Rubenstein, Washington, DC, Washington Institute Press, 1987, p. x.
[4] Dietrich Bonhoeffer, *Letters and Papers from Prison*, ed. E. Bethge, London, SCM, 1967, p.178.
[5] Shupe, *op. cit.*, p.23.
[6] *Study Paper on Religious Liberty: CCIA Background Information*, 1980, no. 4, p.8.
[7] *Ibid.*, pp.9-10.
[8] Hassan-al-Turabi, *New York Times*, 29 January 1992, p.3.
[9] Sahliyeh, *op. cit.*, p.7.
[10] *Ibid.*
[11] Edward Said, quoted from interview in *Time*, 16 April 1979.
[12] George N. Speir, "Letter to the Editor", *New York Times*, 29 January 1992.
[13] Donald Eugene Smith, "The Limits of Religious Resurgence", in *Religious Resurgence and Politics in the Contemporary World, op. cit.*, p.32.
[14] Sahliyeh, *op. cit.*
[15] Theo van Boven, "Advances and Obstacles in Building Understanding and Respect Between People of Diverse Religions and Beliefs", *Human Rights Quarterly*, vol. 13, no. 4, 1991, p.441.
[16] Gabriel Habib, "Misuse of Religious Sentiments, Religion in Conflict Situations", in *Religious Liberty: CCIA Background Information*, 1987, no. 1, p.21.
[17] Allan R. Brockway & J. Paul Rajashekar eds, *New Religious Movements and the Churches*, Geneva, WCC Publications, 1987, p.171.
[18] *Ibid.*, p.184.
[19] James E. Wood Jr, "Religious Pluralism and Religious Freedom", *Journal of Church and State*, vol. 31. no. 1, 1989, p.13.
[20] Dean M. Kelley, "Religious Liberty and Socio-Political Values: Legal Threats to Conversion in the United States", in *New Religious Movements and the Churches, op. cit.*, pp.94-95.
[21] "Summary Statement and Recommendations", in *ibid.*, p.176.
[22] *Ibid.*
[23] The description that follows is from "Religion and Church under Perestroika" by the author in *Perestroika: Some Preliminary Comments: CCIA Background Information*, 1988, no. 1.
[24] Peter Costea, "Church-State Relations in the Marxist-Leninist Regimes of the Third World", *Journal of Church and State*, vol. 32, no. 2, 1990, p.289.

7. The WCC and Religious Liberty

The realities of the world during the period in which the World Council of Churches was formed left a deep imprint on the new ecumenical fellowship. The massive violation of human rights during the second world war challenged the fellowship of the churches to give human rights a high priority on its agenda, and fundamental to these rights was liberty of conscience and belief. It was thus only natural that from the very beginning this became a central concern of the WCC.

The Commission of the Churches on International Affairs (CCIA), which was formed jointly by the International Missionary Council and the World Council of Churches in process of formation, undertook as one of its first tasks to press for international standards on religious liberty. Its director Frederick Nolde played a very active role in lobbying during the preparatory work on the Universal Declaration of Human Rights. The first draft of the article on religious freedom said simply: "There shall be freedom of conscience and belief and of private and public religious worship." The final version, redrafted largely as a result of the work of CCIA, said: "Everyone has the right to freedom of thought, conscience and religion; this right includes freedom to change his religion or belief and freedom either alone or in community with others and in public or private to manifest his religion or belief in teaching, practice, worship and observance."

The fundamental elements of religious liberty, as understood by the World Council of Churches, are clearly stated in the declaration on the topic by the WCC's first assembly (Amsterdam, 1948), to which we have referred several times. In elaborating these elements over the years, the Council was influenced by historical and political changes, the experience of its member churches, the diversity of situations in which the churches live and the kinds of new developments and trends we looked at in the previous chapter. In evaluating the resulting evolution of ecumenical thinking in this area, one must take into account the shift in the prevailing concerns and the expansion in the constituency of the WCC.

The formative period of the WCC was substantially influenced by Western concepts of civil liberty and missionary concerns. The International Missionary Council had done considerable work on religious liberty long before the second world war. Its fundamental emphasis was on the claim for religious freedom in the context of missionary enterprise. The International Missionary Council stated in 1928 at its conference in Jerusalem:

> We call on the followers of non-Christian religions to join with us in the study of Jesus Christ as he stands before us in the scriptures, his place in the life of the world, and his power to satisfy the human heart; to hold fast to faith in the unseen and eternal in the face of the growing materialism of the world; to cooperate with us against all the evils of secularism; to respect freedom of conscience so that men may confess Christ without separation from home and friends; and to discern that all the good of which men have conceived is fulfilled and secured in Jesus Christ.

But the statement also said: "We would repudiate any symptoms of a religious imperialism that would desire to impose beliefs and practices on others in order to manage their souls in their supposed interests."[1]

This was perhaps the first time the question of religious liberty was raised in an international ecumenical forum. The Jerusalem conference saw religious liberty within the context of church-state relations. Major concerns were relations with governments in "non-Christian" lands and freedom for minority churches. One of the conference recommendations called for a study of how religious freedom applies "to the rights of minorities under state systems of education".

The Life and Work movement conference in Oxford in 1937 also considered the question of religious liberty. One of the landmarks of twentieth-century church history, the Oxford conference met under the theme of the relation of the church, state and community, and under the shadow of gathering clouds of war and totalitarianism in Europe. The first announcement of the Oxford conference said its essential theme would be the life-and-death struggle between Christian faith and the secular and pagan tendencies of our time.

The topic of religious liberty arose in the section on "Church and State", which in fact dealt with the freedom of the church. Reflecting on the context of the time, the report referred to four kinds of state:

— a state which is Christian by profession;
— a state where there are majority and minority churches;
— a state which acknowledges a liberal doctrine of rights;
— a state whose constitution and tradition include nothing on the basis of which the church can claim a right.

In the first category "it is self-evident that the church should be free to the fullest extent to fulfill its function", Oxford said. In the second, the same essential liberty to carry out the church's function should be enjoyed by minorities as well as by the majority. In the third category the church, like other associations, should have the liberty which its function requires. The fourth kind of situation does not absolve the church from its primary duty of witness — and this duty must include, under the circumstances, a witness against such a denial of fundamental justice.

Oxford enumerated several freedoms as necessary conditions for the church's fulfillment of its primary duty: the right of public and private worship, preaching and teaching; no state imposition of religious ceremonies and forms of worship; freedom to determine the nature of its government and the qualifications of its ministers and members and, conversely, the freedom of the individual to join the church; control over the education of its ministers, the right to give religious instruction to its youth; freedom of Christian service and missionary activity, both home and foreign, freedom to cooperate with other churches, freedom to use such facilities, open to all citizens or associations, as will make it possible to accomplish these ends.[2]

The Declaration on Religious Liberty by the WCC's first assembly in Amsterdam was easily the best statement of religious liberty of the period. Comprehensive, clear and well-grounded theologically, it was to have considerable influence on discussions of religious liberty around the world. It is true that it reflected perceptions of civil and political rights that were dominant in the West at that time; and it was set in the framework of the concept of the "responsible society" — an ecumenical criterion for evaluating society, influential during the early years of the WCC, which emphasized the accountability of the state to the people.

Several aspects of religious liberty were mentioned in the assembly's report on "The Church and the Disorder of Society".

It condemned "any attempt to limit the freedom of men to obey God and to act according to conscience, for those freedoms are implied in man's responsibility before God". Maintaining that human rights derive directly from the status of human beings as the children of God, the report called it "presumptuous for the state to assume that it can grant or deny fundamental rights". The churches were urged to "support every endeavour to secure within an international bill of rights adequate safeguards for freedom of religion and conscience".

Meeting soon after the disorder of the second world war, the assembly was naturally preoccupied with concern for "a good international order", of which an essential element, said the Declaration on Religious Liberty, is freedom of religion. The WCC thus linked freedom of religion and peace, on the basis of the conviction that freedom of religion is fundamental to all freedoms and that it is only if all freedoms are ensured that peace and a good international order can be established.

The assembly made it clear that in pleading for religious freedom it was not arguing for granting any privilege to Christians that is denied to others. It distinguished between inner freedom and its outward expression. The inner freedom is the liberty Christ has given to human beings and is beyond the purview of any government. But the inner freedom makes Christians "both jealous for its outward expression and solicitous that all men should have freedom in religious life".

As we saw earlier, the Amsterdam declaration stated that religious liberty consists of the following rights:
1. Every person has the right to determine his own faith and creed.
2. Every person has the right to express his religious beliefs in worship, teaching and practice and to proclaim the implications of his beliefs for relationships in a social or political community.
3. Every person has the right to associate with others and to organize with them for religious purposes.
4. Every religious organization formed or maintained by action in accordance with the rights of individual persons, has the right to determine its policies and practices for the accomplishments of its chosen purposes.[3]

In view of the growing international interest in religious liberty, WCC governing bodies felt it necessary to speak on the subject in the two succeeding years. In 1949, the executive committee, meeting in Chichester, UK, in a message to the churches spoke mainly about religious liberty, which was followed a few days later by an action of the central committee on the same subject.

The central concern was about restrictions on religious liberty in many countries of Europe and Asia. The message from the executive committee spoke of hindrances to religious education of young people, prohibition of youth movements, interference with the training of the clergy and appointment of church leaders, obstacles to public evangelism and missionary work and arrests and imprisonment of church officials and members.

The context for this was what was happening in several Eastern European countries and in the People's Republic of China — though the names of the countries were not mentioned. The central committee statement clearly voices the uncertainty and anxiety caused by the revolution in China: "Revolutionary movements are afoot and their end no man can foresee." There is an element of self-criticism of the weakness of the churches' efforts for the underprivileged masses of the world. But the statement rejects any claim by totalitarian methods to bring justice, and it calls on "statesmen and all men who in every nation seek social justice to consider this truth; a peaceful and stable order can only be built upon the foundations of righteousness, of right relations between man and God and between man and man. Only the recognition that man has ends and loyalties beyond the state will ensure true justice to the human person."[4]

The statement affirmed that "religious freedom is the condition and guardian of all true freedom". It was only natural that in the context of some of the measures taken against the church in the revolutionary situations there was a sense of loss of all freedoms. Religious freedom became the test of human rights.

The 1950 central committee meeting in Toronto expressed new concerns in the area of religious liberty. The Chichester statement had mainly dealt with restrictions by states whose policies were antagonistic to religion and its manifestations. To this concern, the Toronto statement added references to restrictions "by dominant religious majorities" and "by religious groups seeking dominance".

The WCC thus recognized that it is not just governments that violate religious liberty but also churches and other agencies. Several instances of restrictions on religious liberty in countries where the Roman Catholic Church was dominant were brought to the attention of the committee. While there were references to "regions in which Muslim faith is the dominant religion" and also to "countries where the Protestants or Orthodox churches were dominant", it was apparent that new major concern was about the Roman Catholic Church.

The second assembly, which met in 1954 in Evanston, outside of Chicago, recognized the absence of several churches because of the political situation and the difficulty of communicating with some of them. It is significant that the tone of its resolution on religious liberty was one of solidarity rather than denunciation, probably in the belief that condemnatory language would only be likely to add to the suffering of the people about whom concerns were being expressed. It therefore recorded its "concern and sorrow" that "in certain countries from which information can be gathered with reasonable accuracy, Christians are suffering many disabilities and even violence; and human rights and liberties, albeit acknowledged in official protestations, have in practice been denied". Being part of the ecumenical fellowship was an important component of religious liberty for the churches, Evanston said.

The central committee which met in Hungary in 1956 received a provisional report on "Christian Witness, Proselytism and Religious Liberty in the Setting of the World Council of Churches". The special commission which prepared this report had been named at Evanston to study "proselytism and religious liberty", in view of difficulties which had arisen affecting relationships between some WCC member churches. The broadening of the title of the study reflected a recognition that proselytism, in its derogatory meaning, represents a corruption of Christian witness or evangelization and underscored that the study's primary focus was a problem affecting the relationship of churches within the WCC. A final report was approved by the third assembly (New Delhi, 1961) after the member churches had an opportunity to comment on the provisional report.

The New Delhi assembly observed that "probably no church and no missionary society involved in the ecumenical movement would wish to call itself a 'proselytizing' body. It does not seem possible, in practice, to restore the good connotation which the word 'proselytize' once carried." The report defined the purpose of witness as persuading "persons to accept the supreme authority of Christ", recognizing that witness and response to it "give rise to problems in the relationship between the churches when one church yields to the temptation to seek its own institutional advantage at the cost of real or seeming disadvantage to another". Proselytism is not something absolutely different from witness, but is the corruption of witness: "Witness is corrupted when cajolery, bribery, undue pressure or intimidation is used — subtly or openly — to bring about seeming conversion."

The issue of proselytism was a central concern of the Orthodox churches, and at the New Delhi assembly several Orthodox churches joined the WCC. But this concern had a fairly long history. The 1920 encyclical of the ecumenical patriarch, with its strong plea for the cooperation among the churches, had asked for a definite cessation of proselytizing activities. At the preliminary meetings of the Faith and Order and Life and Work movements in Geneva, the issue was again brought up by the Orthodox representatives.

The multi-year study on "The Common Christian Responsibility Towards Areas of Rapid Social Change", conducted by the Department of Church and Society beginning in the late 1950s, also addressed issues of religious liberty. The study seemed to reflect Western concerns about the revolutionary events sweeping societies in many parts of the world. It rejected theocracy, which it said was often linked in areas of rapid social change to "oppressive structures and customs of society which are a hindrance to social development". A "neutral state", it said, was most conducive to religious freedom.

But the study admitted that the issue differs from nation to nation. "In some situations, a neutral state is defined as separation of state and political parties from all religions, and in some others as the state's equal concern for all religions. How can we prevent the neutral state being interpreted in terms of dogmas of secularism or of the equality of religions?" The study seemed ambivalent about certain national liberation movements, and asked, "in countries fighting for national freedom, what is the Christian role when the national movements have anti-Christian religious motivations?"

Some years later, the study paper on religious liberty by the WCC's Commission of the Churches on International Affairs (1981)[5] criticized this statement, contrasting its prescriptive nature and limited focus, as well as the methodology of the study itself and "the simplistic context into which the issue of religious liberty is placed", with another ecumenical study of the same period — which was done by the East Asia Christian Conference (precursor of the Christian Conference of Asia) — and included a survey of the traditional social and communal patterns in the various countries in order to understand their relation to religious freedom.

An earlier request for a joint study with the International Missionary Council of "the problems of religious liberty arising in Roman Catholic and other countries" was modified by the central committee meeting in Nyborg in 1958, to call for a study which would articulate "a solidly established basis for our Christian attitude concerning religious freedom". It was the results of this study which were published in 1963 in the book by A.F. Carillo de Albornoz which we have cited several times in earlier chapters — *The Basis of Religious Liberty*. In mandating the study, Nyborg said:

> While there is broad consensus in the ecumenical movement concerning the importance of religious liberty and the need to take a definite stand in its favour, there has not yet emerged a consensus concerning the theological and ethical reasons why religious freedom must be defended. There is need for a comprehensive study of different ideological, religious and political forces which work for religious freedom and of those who work against it.

The New Delhi assembly statement on religious liberties generally followed the Amsterdam declaration. "Holding a distinctive Christian basis for religious liberty," it said, "we regard this right as fundamental for men everywhere." The statement highlighted the significance of religious witness and practice in political and social life as an element of religious liberty by elaborating on the freedom to manifest one's belief:

> It includes freedom to worship according to one's chosen form, in public or in private. It includes freedom to teach, whether by formal or informal instruction, as well as preaching with a view to propagating one's faith and persuading others to accept it. It includes freedom to practise religion or belief, whether by performance of acts of mercy or by the expression, word or deed of the implications of belief in social, economic and political matters both domestic and international.

At its meeting in 1966, the WCC central committee welcomed "with satisfaction the Vatican Council's Declaration on Religious Liberty, with its clear statement proclaiming full civil religious freedom, both individual and collective for everybody everywhere". It did, however, point out that "there are certain aspects of the... declaration with which we cannot fully agree". (We shall return to the Vatican declaration in greater detail in the next chapter.)

By the time of the Uppsala assembly in 1968 the WCC's understanding of human rights had broadened, and the assembly stated that "churches should strive to make their congregations feel that in the modern worldwide community the rights of the individual are inevitably bound up with the struggle for a better standard of living for the underprivileged of all nations". It also said that "the full application of religious liberty to individuals and organizations and the free right of expression of conscience for all persons is fundamentally important for all human freedoms".

The years following the Uppsala assembly featured an intense debate on human rights in the context of struggles for justice. During this period there was a clear shift in the WCC's programmes towards actions in support of such struggles; and reflection on these experiences added a new dimension to the understanding of human rights. In particular the experiences of the churches in Asia, Africa and Latin America influenced the World Council of Churches more than in previous periods. The special situation of the churches in Eastern Europe also had to be taken into account, as they entered the ecumenical discussion on human rights for the first time.

A 1974 consultation on "Human Rights and Christian Responsibility" in St Pölten, Austria, attempted to forge a new ecumenical consensus on human rights which would place the issue of religious liberty squarely within the framework of human rights as a whole. The report of the consultation, recalling that the WCC had often declared religious liberty to be a basic human right, insisted that "this right is required so that the full responsibilities of Christian faith may be undertaken. This right is not a privilege or exclusive freedom for the church. Human solidarity demands that we should be aware of the interrelatedness of all rights including the rights of those of other faiths or no faiths... The right to religious liberty exists in order to serve the community according to the commands of the gospel."

The findings of this consultation became the basis for the report of the fifth assembly the next year in Nairobi. Affirming that human rights have to be seen in the context of Christian responsibility and solidarity, Nairobi said that

> the gospel leads us to become ever more active in identifying and rectifying violations of human rights in our own societies, and to enter into new forms of ecumenical solidarity with Christians elsewhere who are similarly engaged. It leads us into the struggle of the poor and the oppressed both within and outside the church as they seek to achieve their full human rights, and presses us to work together with people of other faiths or ideologies who share with us a common concern for human dignity...
>
> The right to religious freedom has been and continues to be a major concern of member churches and the World Council of Churches. However this right should not be seen as belonging exclusively to the church. This right is inseparable from other fundamental human rights. No religious community should plead for its own religious liberty without active respect and reverence for the faith and basic human rights of others... Religious liberty should never be used to claim privileges. For the church this right is essential so that it can fulfill its responsibilities which arise out of the Christian faith...
>
> Religious freedom should also include the right and duty of religious bodies to criticize the ruling powers when necessary, on the basis of their religious convictions. In this context, it was noted that many Christians in different parts of the world are in prison for reasons of conscience or for political reasons as a result of their seeking to respond to the total demands of the gospel.

The statement on religious liberty issued by the executive committee in 1979 recognized "a progressive evolution in the ecumenical understanding of religious liberty, which has been augmented and refined by the variety of concrete experiences of member churches as they live and work in vastly different environments". Rather than viewing religious liberty as a static principle that need only to be applied according to internationally recognized standards of behaviour, the executive committee felt "the need for a constant review of a fast changing scene, as also for a vigilant pastoral concern, not only for all whose liberties are curtailed but also for those elements within all ideological systems and religious leaderships who are earnestly seeking a reinterpretation along more human lines of previous judgments on the human rights of those who disagree with them on religious grounds".

We have already cited several times the 1981 *Study Paper on Religious Liberty* by the CCIA. After tracing how ecumenical positions on religious liberty have evolved and noting reasons for a renewed concern on the issue, the study paper said: "Viewed in isolation, the various concrete examples of situations where religious liberty is seen to be limited or curtailed do not represent totally new or unique phenomena. Of course, it is clear that even those issues and situations which have not substantially changed over the years need continued attention and even renewed approaches. And yet, the 'context' and framework in which Christians find themselves dealing with the issue has changed."

The paper identified several areas where religious liberty problems are found. In countries undergoing radical transformation, accompanied by new juridical relations between the state and the religious communities, churches have experienced difficulties. In some countries Christians and people of other faiths have sometimes experienced problems in maintaining relations with and receiving support from co-religionists and organizations from outside. New practical and theological questions regarding religious liberty are raised when Christians have become actively involved in struggles for justice and human rights. Complicity of some churches and religious communities with the economic, political and ideological structures of certain societies has contributed to the curtailment of religious liberty.

Minority religious communities have suffered in situations where communal and national aspirations are defined in religious terms.

Past discussions of religious liberty were too much influenced by ideological considerations arising out of the East-West rivalry, the paper suggested. An important question now was "whether the patterns of political, social, economic and cultural life as evolved in the North are necessarily the only or the most suitable basis on which the future of the world society is to be constructed".

Religious liberty found a prominent place in the statement on human rights by the WCC's sixth assembly (Vancouver, 1983). The statement identified the threat to religious freedom from the growing climate of religious fanaticism and the rise of political fundamentalism. While welcoming the adoption of the UN Declaration on the Elimination of All Forms of Intolerance and of Discrimination Based on Religion or Belief, the assembly expressed the fear that it did not "offer sufficient protection against specific problems facing religious communities today... It is therefore imperative that member churches and the WCC continue to identify and denounce gross violations of religious freedom and extend moral and material assistance to those who suffer oppression and even persecution because of their religious beliefs and practices."

CCIA's human rights advisory group addressed the issue of religious liberty against the background of tensions and conflicts in several multi-religious situations, the important role played by Christians in social and political struggles on the basis of their faith and renewed attempts within the UN system for a binding instrument on religious freedom. The WCC's conciliar process on Justice, Peace and Integrity of Creation had as one of its basic assumptions the conviction that the churches' engagement in struggles for liberation, justice and human dignity should not be just one of the activities of the church but part of its confession of faith.

Examining limitations on religious liberty experienced in some societies, the advisory group suggested guidelines and criteria for legitimate limits to religious practice and witness, emphasizing that assessment of such limitations could only be done properly by understanding their concrete contexts. Limitations which look similar on the face of it may in practice work out quite differently according to the social and legal context in which they are applied.

The advisory group also considered the qustion of whether a special plea or defence can be made of social or political action on the basis of religious convictions. (This is not the same as civil disobedience — disobeying a law out of Christian motivation and bearing the legal consequences as a form of witness or an expression of solidarity.) Without giving a clear-cut answer to this question, the advisory group did say that from a Christian point of view no authority, civil or otherwise, can impede a Christian from pleading on religious grounds. But the line between religious-based pleas or defences and expressions of bigotry or outright fanaticism may sometimes be very thin. If a law as such is based on religion, the question may rather be whether it is feasible to make the plea on secular understandings or convictions.

NOTES

[1] Statement of the International Missionary Council, Jerusalem, 1928, in *The Christian Life and Message in Relation to Non-Christian Systems*, vol. 1, London, Oxford University Press, 1928, p.491 and 484.
[2] *The Churches Survey Their Task*, report of the Oxford conference on "Church, Community and State", London, George Allen & Unwin, 1937, pp.84-85.
[3] Declaration on Religious Liberty, assembly of the WCC, Amsterdam, 1948.
[4] Statement of the central committee, WCC, Chichester, 1949.
[5] *Study Paper on Religious Liberty: CCIA Background Information*, 1981, no. 4.

8. The Roman Catholic Church and Religious Liberty

> Justice therefore forbids, and reason itself forbids, the state to be godless; or to adopt a line of action which would end in godlessness — namely, to treat the various religions (as they call them) alike, and to bestow upon them promiscuously equal rights and privileges. Since, then, the profession of one religion is necessary in the state, that religion must be professed which alone is true.
>
> Pope Leo XIII (1888)

> Religious freedom, an essential element of the dignity of every person, is a cornerstone of the structure of human rights, and for this reason an irreplaceable factor in the good of individuals and of the whole of society, as well as the personal fulfilment of each individual. It follows that the freedom of individuals and of communities to profess and practise their religion is an essential element for peaceful human existence.   Pope John Paul II (1988)

During the hundred years between those statements by the two popes, the Roman Catholic Church travelled a long way from being a main violator of religious freedom to becoming a major champion of religious freedom. The turning point was the Second Vatican Council in 1965.

Before the 1960s Roman Catholic views on religious freedom oscillated between the thesis that there is no religious liberty for those "in error" and the hypothesis that religious liberty can be provisionally granted to non-Catholics when the common good makes it advisable and complete repression of erroneous beliefs is not practicable. To many this appeared to be sheer opportunism: a willingness to tolerate religious liberty for practical reasons, while maintaining that the ideal is the denial of religious liberty and the union of all in one Catholic faith. In practice, religious liberty was denied where Catholics were the overwhelming majority, but upheld where Catholics were in the minority. Historical circumstances played a significant part in the development of Roman Catholic thinking in favour of religious liberty, but it was a gradual evolution.

While Pius XI (1922-39) affirmed that "man as a person possesses God-given rights", he did not extend these to the realm of religious liberty, and actually rejected the expression "liberty of conscience" as equivocal. According to him "absolute independence of conscience" was "absurd for a soul created and redeemed by God".

The Roman Catholic rejection of religious liberty before Vatican II must be seen in the light of its opposition to what was called modern liberalism with its emphasis on liberty in all its forms. In the nineteenth century, individualistic liberalism, with its emphasis on freedom, was seen as the primary problem of the age, unacceptable to the Roman Catholic Church. The way in which the Catholic church understood the relation of the paternal state to religious freedom was not designed for, nor applicable to, a responsible democracy. But after the first world war, the rise of twentieth-century totalitarianism posed new problems; and the Catholic church came to see the need to defend the dignity and rights of human persons.

Nevertheless, as Beach points out, even as late as the 1950s the Vatican was not prepared to defend religious freedom equally for all. He draws certain principles out of a 1953 speech by Pope Pius XII to Italian jurists: "(1) Only Catholics have the right to religious liberty as 'human beings' (natural law) 'because' they have the truth; (2) non-Catholics may have the right to religious liberty as 'citizens' because of legal norms promoting the 'common good'... Basically we are back to the late nineteenth-century papal position of toleration."[1]

Roman Catholic theologian Richard J. Regan explains that "despite the fact that Pius perceived in the transition of modern society from paternal to democratic principles even a natural postulate of reason, and despite the fact that he defended the rights of the persons against the claims of totalitarian governments, he did not explicitly affirm religious freedom as a human right".[2]

The clear departure in favour of religious liberty was made by John XXIII. In his encyclical *Pacem in Terris* he emphasized human dignity and recognized resulting human rights and duties as inviolable and inalienable. The encyclical said that "every human being has the right to honour God according to the dictates of an upright conscience, and the right to profess his religion privately and publicly".

As Regan comments, "John XXIII seemed to draw from Pius XII's premises the unqualified conclusion that religious freedom is a right proper to the human person. In one sentence of one encyclical, John appeared to work a veritable Copernican revolution in the theology of religious freedom."[3]

The Declaration on Religious Freedom, adopted by the Second Vatican Council on 7 December 1965, was apparently the most difficult document of the Council, with the draft going through several revisions over a long period. Formidable opposition came from a conservative minority who articulated the classic position that since the Catholic church is the unique instrument of God's plan for salvation, a "Catholic" state has the duty to protect its citizens from religious error, if needed by using coercive power. On this view, a Catholic state could never accept as a principle the right of all individuals and groups to the freedom of religious exercise; it can only tolerate public non-Catholic religious exercises as a matter of practice.

The majority, however, though differing in how they saw the basis of religious liberty, marshalled arguments in support of the affirmation of the principle of religious freedom.

At the outset, the Declaration identifies its subject as the right of the individual and of communities to social and civic freedom in religious matters. It is not about "inner freedom" or "freedom in Christ" but about social and civic freedom, commonly known as religious liberty. Acknowledging the increasing demands for freedom in modern times, it says these "chiefly concern the quest for the values proper to the human spirit" and, "in the first place, the free exercise of religion in society".

Since Catholics believe that the one true religion subsists in the catholic and apostolic church, the Declaration asserts that "all men are bound to seek the truth especially in what concerns God and his church, to embrace the truth they come to know of and to hold fast to it". Religious freedom, it continues, which is required so that people can fulfill their duty to worship God, has to do with immunity from coercion in civil society. The traditional Catholic doctrine of the moral duty of people and societies towards the true religion and towards the one church of Christ is thus left untouched.

This section on "one true religion" was designed both to satisfy the conservatives and to maintain doctrinal continuity. It was not possible to have a document which would even indirectly repudiate traditional Catholic doctrine. It may also be argued that the Declaration does not deny religious truth outside the Catholic church. This section is about what "we believe". But was it necessary to propound this particular belief in this document? Beach argues that "the claim that the Roman Catholic Church possesses the 'unique true religion' is quite irrelevant to civil liberty in religious matters, and this does not fit in with a declaration regarding religious liberty in 'social' and 'civil' spheres".[4]

Under the heading of the "general nature of religious freedom", the Council declared that "the human person has a right to religious freedom" and that this right "has its foundation in the very dignity of the human person as this dignity is known through the revealed word of God and by reason itself".

The church is following the way of Christ and the apostles when it recognizes and supports the principle of religious freedom in this way, according to the Declaration. While claiming that "throughout the ages the church has preserved and handed on the doctrine received from the Master and from the apostles" there is an element of mild self-criticism in the admission that "in the life of the people of God, as they have made their pilgrim way through the vicissitudes of human history, a way of acting has sometimes appeared that was hardly in accord with the spirit of the gospel, or was even opposed to it". This reference to the fortunes of religious freedom within the history of Christianity and the tacit concession that the Catholic church has sometimes used coercion to achieve secular ends broaches a delicate issue. But the Declaration distinguishes between doctrine and practice, affirming that "the church's doctrine that no one is to be coerced into faith has always stood firm".

Its statement that it is pre-eminent that "the church should enjoy that full measure of freedom which her care for the salvation of men requires" appears to call for special privilege of the church. "The freedom of the church is the fundamental principle in relations between the church and governments and the whole civil order." But the Declaration also says that "a harmony exists between the freedom of the church and the religious freedom which is to be recognized as the right of all men and communities and to be sanctioned by constitutional law".

It maintains that civil authority has no jurisdiction over religious acts. "The religious acts whereby men, in private and in public and out of a sense of personal conviction, direct their lives to God transcend by their very nature the order of terrestrial and temporal affairs. It would clearly transgress the limits set to its power were it to presume to direct or inhibit acts that are religious." But the civil authorities do have specific obligations, which the Declaration spells out in some detail. Probably to avoid the complexity of "church-state" issues, the Declaration uses the terms "civil authority", "civil society" and "government" rather than the term "state".

Certain matters are outside the competence of a government. If it were to presume to direct or inhibit acts that are religious, it would be going beyond its competence. A government is wrong when it imposes upon its people, by force or fear or other means, the profession or repudiation of any religion, when it hinders people from joining or leaving a religious community. It is a violation of God's will for a government to use force to destroy or repress religion.

Since an essential duty of government is to protect and promote inviolable human rights, "the government is to undertake the protection of the religious freedom of all its citizens, in an effective manner, by just laws and by other appropriate means". It also has the duty to see that "the equality of citizens before the law is never violated, whether openly or covertly, for religious reasons."

In dealing with the issue of possible limitations on religious liberty by the civil authority, the Declaration uses the expression "moderating norms" and with reference to civil authority speaks mainly of judicial norms. Society, it says, "has the right to defend itself against possible abuses committed on pretext of freedom of religion". Laws to protect public order, however, should not be arbitrary or unfairly partisan, but should be "controlled by juridical norms which are in conformity with objective moral order". Admittedly, "public order" is a rather elastic concept, but it is widely used even though subject to misuse by civil authorities; and the Declaration cannot be criticized on the ground that it refers to the concept.

Several Catholic commentators have pointed to a number of ambiguities in the Declaration's application of the principle of religious freedom. Regan points out that its condemnation of proselytism "is couched in unspecific and non-objective language".[5] The Declaration says that "in spreading religious faith and in introducing religious practices, everyone ought at all times to refrain from any manner of action which might seem to carry a hint of coercion or of a kind of persuasion that would be dishonourable or dishonest or unworthy". This, he says, appears to yield too much, and civil authorities could appeal to phrases like "hint of coercion" and "dishonesty" to take actions which violate religious liberty.

A comment in the Declaration about state churches has also been debated. It says: "If, in view of peculiar circumstances obtaining in nations, special recognition is given to one religious community in the constitutional order of society, it is at the same time imperative that the right of all citizens and religious communities to religious freedom should be recognized and made effective in practice." It could be argued that in such a situation, citizens do *not* have equal religious freedom and that the state or established church enjoys privileges not extended to others. Moreover, such situations raise the risk of compromise with the state by the church concerned, which thus actually gives up part of its religious liberty for the sake of some privileges.

The argument in favour of including such a comment in the Declaration is that it does not make any value judgment about the special situation it describes. It says only that if such a situation exists the religious freedom of all must be recognized and protected. It can also be argued that the statement can apply to any situation in which one religious confession — Anglican, Lutheran, Orthodox — has such special recognition, and that the Declaration was not defending any special privilege of the Catholic church. Nevertheless, many would challenge the obvious implication of the statement that special civil recognition of a religion or having an established church is compatible in theory with full religious freedom.

Surprisingly, the Declaration is not explicit about the right to change one's creed and does not seem to recognize the practical importance of this issue.

As Regan points out, "the Declaration's affirmation of the principle of religious freedom posed a difficult problem in the development of doctrine, since no one could deny the *prima-facie* adverse position of the nineteenth-century papacy on the issue. Of course, from the purely juridical point of view, the church had never definitely accepted the nineteenth-century papal position and could, therefore, reverse that position without abandoning any article of faith." But, Regan says, that argument ignores "the dynamic historical process in which the church progressively articulates her consciousness of the word of God... The Declaration on Religious Freedom recognizes the inadequacy and inaccuracy of Leo XIII's theology."[6]

Despite its shortcomings, the Vatican II Declaration on Religious Freedom stands as a landmark in the universal church's quest for freedom. That its proclamation of religious freedom came as a doctrine of the Catholic church in a solemn and authoritative way by a council in union with the pope heightened its significance. While the impact of the Declaration cannot be easily assessed, subsequent legislative and constitutional changes — though not in full conformity with religious freedom — in such predominantly Catholic countries as Spain and Italy could be directly attributed to the Declaration.

The Vatican elaborated its principles on religious liberty in a memorandum to the follow-up to the 1975 Helsinki Conference on Security and Cooperation in Europe, held in Madrid in 1980. It gave a list of elements considered necessary in order to achieve full religious liberty at the personal, community and international levels.

A more extensive elaboration of contemporary Roman Catholic thinking on religious liberty came in 1988, when Pope John Paul II made religious freedom the theme of his message for the celebration of the world day of peace. That message went beyond the Declaration on several points and for the most part corresponds closely to positions taken by the World Council of Churches. Its opening statement is cited at the head of this chapter.

The link between religious freedom and peace is clearly articulated in the papal message. "Every violation of religious freedom, whether open or hidden," said John Paul II, "does fundamental damage to the cause of peace, like violations of the other fundamental rights of the human person."[7] He echoes the affirmation of the Declaration that the inalienable rights of the human person are not conferred from outside or subject to any external constraint.

At the time of Vatican II, the Roman Catholic Church was still uncomfortable with the terminology of human rights, and the Declaration on Religious Freedom did not not give much emphasis to the relationship of religious freedom to other human rights. By contrast, the 1988 papal message uses the language of human rights and says "that the civil and political right to religious freedom, inasmuch as it touches the most intimate sphere of the spirit, is a point of reference of the other fundamental rights and in some way becomes a measure of them", adding that civil authorities have the duty of ensuring that both the rights of individuals and of communities and proper public order are safeguarded.[8]

Unlike the Declaration, the message uses the term "state" in addition to "civil authorities". The question of religions having special recognition is taken up again ("even in cases where the state grants a special juridical position to a particular religion, there is a duty to ensure that the right to freedom of conscience is legally recognized and effectively respected for all citizens"[9]), but if these words sounded in 1965 like a justification of Catholic states, by 1988 they seem to be a defence of religious liberty of Christians and others in Islamic states.

Freedom of conscience was the theme of the pope's world day of peace message in 1991, which began: "If you want peace, respect the conscience of every person."[10] Events in Eastern and Central Europe were very much in the pope's mind: "The need to take concrete steps towards ensuring full respect for freedom of conscience, both legally and in ordinary human relations, has become even more urgent in the light of the events of last year."

The pope is quite unequivocal about the freedom of conscience. "No human authority has the right to interfere with a person's conscience. Conscience bears witness to the transcendence of the person, also in regard to society at large, and as such is inviolable." While repeating the mild self-critical remarks of the Roman Catholic Church's denial of religious freedom (from the Vatican II Declaration), the pope says: "A serious threat to peace is posed by intolerance, which manifests itself in the denial of freedom of conscience to others... In public life, intolerance leaves no room for a plurality of political or social options and thus imposes a monolithic vision of civil and cultural life."

Perhaps again with the situation of Eastern Europe in mind, the Pope links the issue of intolerance with the plight of the minorities. "Much remains to be done to overcome religious intolerance, which in different parts of the world is closely connected with the oppression of minorities. Unfortunately, we are still witnessing attempts to impose a particular religious idea on others, either directly by a proselytism which relies on means which are truly coercive or indirectly by the denial of certain civil or political rights."

The intimate relationship between freedom of conscience and freedom of religion is easily proved because "objectively speaking the search for truth and the search for God are one and the same. It also explains why the systematic denial of God and the establishment of a regime which incorporates this denial in its very constitution are dramatically opposed to both freedom of conscience and freedom of religion."

Fundamentalism is also identified as a threat to tolerance. "Fundamentalism can lead to the exclusion of others from civil society; where religion is concerned it can lead to forced 'conversion'."

It is not sufficient to "protect" minorities by reducing them to the category of wards of the state or those who have not yet reached adulthood. "Rather the inalienable right to follow one's conscience and to profess and practise one's own faith individually or within a community is to be acknowledged and guaranteed, always provided that the demands of public order are not violated."

The tone of the message is considerably influenced by the consciousness that in the pluralistic world in which we live, respect for everyone's conscience is an urgent need.

Reiterating that "religious freedom is not merely one human right among others", the 1991 message affirms that "it is the most fundamental, since the dignity of every person has its first source in his essential relationship with God, the Creator and the Father, in whose image and likeness he was created and since he is endowed with intelligence and freedom. Religious freedom is the most profound expression of freedom of conscience."

NOTES

[1] Bert B. Beach, *Bright Candle of Courage*, Boise, Idaho, Pacific Press Publishing Association, 1989, p.80.
[2] Richard J. Regan, *Conflict and Consensus — Religious Freedom and the Second Vatican Council*, New York, Macmillan, 1967, p.9.
[3] *Ibid.*
[4] Beach, *op. cit.*, p.84.
[5] Regan, *op. cit.*, p.174.
[6] *Ibid.*, p.177.
[7] Message of His Holiness Pope John Paul II for the world day of peace, 1 January 1988.
[8] *Ibid.*
[9] *Ibid.*
[10] Message of His Holiness Pope John Paul II for the world day of peace, 1 January 1991.

9. The United Nations and Religious Liberty

One of the main purposes of the United Nations is "to achieve international cooperation in solving international problems of an economic, social, cultural or humanitarian character and in promoting and encouraging respect for human rights and for fundamental freedoms for all without distinction as to race, sex, language or religion". In those provisions of the UN charter concerned with discrimination, religion is consistently specified along with race, sex and language as an impermissible ground of differentiation.

This objective is also set forth in the preamble to the Universal Declaration of Human Rights, which recalls the words of Franklin Roosevelt in describing the "advent of a world in which human beings shall enjoy freedom of speech and belief and freedom from fear and want... as the highest aspiration of the common people". The first part of the Declaration rejects any discrimination on the basis of religion in stipulating that "everyone is entitled to all the rights and freedoms set forth in this Declaration, without distinction of any kind".

The Universal Declaration has become an important part of international law and has been instrumental in setting international norms and national legislation. Article 1, proclaiming that all human beings are "endowed with reason and conscience and should act towards one another in a spirit of brotherhood", asserts a belief in the human ability to act together rationally to achieve a better state for humankind. Article 18, which deals specifically with religious liberty, may be quoted again here: "Everyone has the right to freedom of thought, conscience and religion; this right includes freedom to change his religion or belief, and freedom, either alone or in community with others and in public or private, to manifest his religion or belief in teaching, practice, worship and observance."

The most debated part of this description was that relating to the freedom to change religion or belief. Traditional Muslim law maintains severe rules against "apostasy", and the representative of Saudi Arabia called this article of the Universal Declaration the result of a common plot of some missionary religions. The representative of Pakistan, however, took another view. He said: "Islam is a missionary religion. It claims the right and the freedom to persuade any man to change his faith and accept Islam. Surely and obviously, it must equally yield to other faiths the free right of conversion. It would be most unreasonable to claim (for oneself) the right of conversion and deny it to others."[1] The issue was bound to come up at every stage of further formulations on religious liberty by the United Nations.

The next stage was the adoption by the United Nations general assembly in 1966 and the entry into force in 1976 of the International Covenant on Economic, Social and Cultural Rights, the International Covenant on Civil and Political Rights and the Optional Protocol to the latter, relating to the right of individual petition. Theo van Boven notes that while these covenants provide for the suspension of many human rights obligations in time of public emergency, they explicitly forbid suspension of the right to life, the right to freedom of thought, conscience and religion and the prohibition of torture and slavery. The Covenant on Economic, Social and Cultural Rights stipulates that "education shall promote understanding, tolerance and friendship among all nations and all racial, ethnic or religious groups" and binds states to respect the liberty of parents "to ensure the religious and moral education of their children in conformity with their own convictions".[2]

The Covenant on Civil and Political Rights does not explicitly provide for the right to change one's religion. Instead, it refers to a person's "freedom to have or to adopt a religion or belief of his choice". This slight difference was due to reservations by some Islamic states, which opposed an explicit right to change one's belief. But one may argue that this formulation does not compromise the freedom to change one's religion, for to be free to have or adopt a religion or belief of one's choice implies the freedom to change one's religion or belief.

Freedom of religion — or at least tolerance — was central in the attempts by the League of Nations to draft the earliest international human rights laws, already before the second world war. But moving from the general principles of the UN charter and the Universal Declaration of Human Rights to the specific covenants touched on many sensitive issues, and progress was slow. Natan Lerner describes the process as "an interesting exposure of UN politics".[3]

In 1960 the UN was asked to take a stand concerning the outburst of anti-semite incidents ("Swastika epidemics") in Europe and elsewhere. This led to adoption of a number of resolutions by UN human rights bodies expressing concern about the manifestation of anti-semitism and other forms of racial prejudice and religious intolerance. It was perhaps natural that these discussions would lead to wider consideration of issues of discrimination based on race or religion. Several African countries proposed the preparation of an international convention on eliminating all forms of racial discrimination. Finally the general assembly adopted two separate resolutions, one calling for preparation of a draft declaration and convention on eliminating discrimination and the other for drafts on the elimination of religious intolerance.

Lerner says this decision was meant as a compromise to eliminate opposition from communist and Arab delegations to an instrument that would cover both the religious and racist aspects. "The East European socialist states wanted to avoid a full discussion on religious matters; the Arabs were anxious to play down anti-semitism. The influence of the Afro-Asian delegations, who were not interested in the religious question, combined with the attitude of the above-mentioned two blocs of countries, was decisive in downgrading work on instruments dealing with religion."[4]

Already in 1956 the Sub-Commission on Prevention of Discrimination and Protection of Minorities had appointed Arcot Krishnaswamy as special rapporteur for a study of discrimination in the matter of religious rights and practices. When the Sub-Commission discussed the text of the study in 1960, it was praised as an exceptionally comprehensive and constructive study which would remain for many years the classic work in an extremely delicate and controversial field, and which would serve as a guide for action by governments, non-governmental organizations and private individuals. The Krishnaswamy study reflected considerable scholarship and sensitivity of a very high order.

In 1962 the general assembly asked the Economic and Social Council (ECOSOC) to draft both a declaration and convention on the elimination of all forms of religious intolerance. The Sub-Commission prepared drafts of both, but in 1972 the general assembly decided to give priority to completing the declaration before resuming consideration of the convention, thereby effectively shelving a mandatory treaty for an indefinite period. In 1973 the general assembly affirmed the equal importance of the proposed declaration and convention, and in 1974 it requested the Commission to submit to it a single draft declaration.

The Commission completed this work only in 1981. Religious and other non-governmental organizations played an important part in persuading several governments in the adoption of the draft. Later that year the general assembly adopted the Declaration on the Elimination of All Forms of Intolerance and of Discrimination Based on Religion or Belief.

Although the drafting process had been virtually deadlocked at times, van Boven says, "the Declaration did finally emerge as a valuable set of norms, which lends itself as a yardstick to measure compliance by governments and as a tool to promote respect and tolerance... The study and basic rules formulated by Krishnaswamy and the draft principles which the Sub-Commission drew up on the basis of these rules had a substantial impact on the text and the outlook of the Declaration."[5]

Krishnaswamy referred throughout his report to "freedom of thought, conscience and religion". The terminology now in vogue is "freedom of thought, conscience, religion *or belief*". It is generally agreed that "religion or belief" includes theistic, non-theistic and atheistic beliefs. Krishnaswamy did not examine the question of intolerance based on religion or belief in his study, being limited by his terms of reference to the question of discrimination in the matter of religious rights and practices. The question of intolerance was introduced by the general assembly only in 1967, when it changed the title of the draft convention to include that term.

Article 2 contains this definition of intolerance and discrimination:

> "Intolerance and discrimination based on religion or belief" means any distinction, exclusion, restriction or preference based on religion or belief and having as its purpose or as its effect nullification or impairment of the recognition, enjoyment or exercise of human rights and fundamental freedoms on an equal basis.

During the discussion major difficulties arose particularly on three issues: the right to change religion, the introduction of the phrase "whatever belief" and the definition of religious freedom. Some Islamic states asserted again that they could not accept the guarantee of an individual's right to change religion.

An Iranian representative attacked the "malicious secularism of the United Nations". Several socialist states complained of the lack of explicit recognition that the rights of atheists and non-theists are equal to those of the religiously faithful. As a result, when the draft declaration was finalized in the general assembly, the reference to the freedom to adopt or change religion was deleted and a clause was added to the effect that nothing stated in the Universal Declaration of Human Rights was to be diminished by the new Declaration. The reference to freedom of religion of "whatever belief" was to accommodate the views of the socialist states. The Declaration does not contain any definition of words such as "religion", "practice" or "observance".

B.R. Ramcharan points out that there has been "a 'downward thrust' in the drafting process: whereas the Universal Declaration referred to the freedom to 'change' religion or belief, the Covenant referred to the freedom to 'have and adopt' religion, while the Declaration refers only to the freedom to have and to manifest religion".[6] The parameters of the right to change one's religion or belief thus remain uncertain. In 1986, however, the Rapporteur of a later study by the Sub-Commission, Elizabeth Odio Benito, concluded after careful examination that although these provisions varied slightly in wording, "all meant precisely the same thing: that everyone has the right to leave one religion or belief and to adopt another, or to remain without any at all". In her view, this interpretation is implicit in the right to freedom of thought, conscience, religion or belief — no matter how that concept is presented.[7]

As we have noted earlier, the freedom of thought, conscience and religion set forth in article 1 of the Declaration must be distinguished from the freedom to manifest religion or belief. No limitations upon the freedom of thought and the freedom to have a religion or belief are permissible. In contrast, the freedom to manifest one's religion or belief may be subject to restraints designed to protect other human rights and the various interests of society. The only restraints permitted by the Declaration are those prescribed by law and necessary to protect public safety, order, health or morals and the fundamental rights and freedoms of others. But these terms are broad and vague.

Analysis of specific restrictions must be alert to interpretations that would weaken the safeguards created and magnify uncertainties concerning the resolution of conflicts.

Among the grounds for recognized restrictions, "public morals" and the "fundamental rights and freedoms of others" bear a particularly important relationship to the freedom of religion or belief. The former category may, because of the inherent vagueness of the concept of morality, be abused to challenge the principles upon which the Declaration is based through attacks on the expression of beliefs and practices that diverge from the norms or values of the majority. As to the latter, it may be argued that the range of human rights that will serve as legitimate bases for restrictions should include only those human rights considered to be "fundamental". But it should be noted that the terms "human rights" and "fundamental rights" are used interchangeably in international and regional human rights instruments.

Article 6 of the Declaration provides a detailed list of what is included in the right to freedom of thought, conscience, religion or belief:

- To worship or assemble in connection with a religion or belief and to establish and maintain places for these purposes.
- To establish and maintain appropriate charitable or humanitarian institutions.
- To make, acquire and use to an adequate extent the necessary articles and materials related to the rites or customs of a religion or belief.
- To write, issue and disseminate relevant publications in these areas.
- To teach a religion or belief in places suitable for these purposes.
- To solicit and receive voluntary financial and other contributions from individuals and institutions.
- To train, appoint, elect or designate by succession appropriate leaders called for by the requirements and standards of any religion or belief.
- To observe days of rest and celebrate holidays and ceremonies in accordance with the precepts of one's religion or belief.
- To establish and maintain communications with individuals and communities in matters of religion and belief at the national and international levels.

It is important to point out that this article deals with individual as well as collective rights and rights that can only be exercised by the group as such. Human rights instruments in the UN system do not generally deal with group rights. In addition to the right to establish and maintain places for worship and to appoint leaders, the article includes another collective right of great importance — that of maintaining communications with individuals and communities of the same religion or belief.

The obligations of states are set forth in articles 4 and 7. They must take effective measures to prevent and eliminate discrimination on the grounds of religion or belief "in the recognition, exercise and enjoyment of human rights and fundamental freedoms in all fields of civil, economic, political and cultural life". Where necessary they must enact or rescind legislation in order to prohibit such discrimination. Article 7 says the rights and freedoms set forth in the Declaration "shall be accorded in national legislation in such a manner that everyone shall be able to avail himself of such rights and freedoms in practice". The wording here seems to make this less binding on the states than the provisions in article 4.

In 1982 the general assembly adopted a resolution requesting the Commission on Human Rights to consider measures necessary to implement the Declaration. The Commission in turn asked its Sub-Commission for "a comprehensive and thorough study of the current dimensions of the problems of intolerance and of discrimination on grounds of religion or belief" using the Declaration as terms of reference. The Special Rapporteur of this study was Elizabeth Odio Benito.

She concluded that the term "intolerance and discrimination based on religion or belief" encompasses not only discrimination infringing upon or negating the right to freedom of thought, conscience, religion and belief, but also acts which stir up hatred against or persecution of such persons or groups. Intolerance and discrimination may arise between religions or between beliefs within a religion as well as between the state and religions and beliefs and between individuals or groups of different religions or beliefs or within nations. Among the proposals for action by the United Nations, governments and non-governmental organizations in the final report, submitted in 1986, was one for the drafting of an international convention on religious intolerance.[8] This would involve submission of reports and establishment of specialized committees to consider them.

In 1988 the Sub-Commission asked Theo van Boven to undertake a study of the "issues and factors which should be considered before any drafting of a further binding international instrument on freedom of religion or belief takes place".

Without attempting to give an explicit answer to the question whether it was desirable or not to draft a convention, van Boven enumerated certain issues and factors to be considered. A new instrument, he wrote, can never serve as an excuse for failure to implement already existing standards; and any further binding instrument should build on the standards already elaborated by the international community. He also referred to the proliferation of implementation committees under international human rights treaties and the inadequate resources within the United Nations to service these committees. In conclusion, he said: "The overall thrust of this paper is the need for solid work, on the basis of sound research and careful analysis, if it were decided to draft a further binding international instrument on freedom of religion or belief."[9]

We have already noted a "downward thrust" in the process of drafting on religious liberty in the United Nations system. There is a genuine risk that drafting a binding instrument might weaken rather than strengthen international guarantees of religious liberty.

Human rights practices of states take place within the broader context of an international human rights regime centred on the United Nations. The principles of this regime are the rights listed in the Universal Declaration of Human Rights. These rights are further elaborated in the two International Covenants on Economic, Social and Cultural Rights and on Civil and Political Rights. For states which have signed and ratified them, these are treaties to which they are parties. In addition, there are conventions — which are also treaties for the signatories — on particular issues such as racial discrimination, the rights of women, and torture; these covenants and the conventions are legislation and form part of international law. They are binding upon the parties.

Strictly speaking, the Universal Declaration of Human Rights as such does not have the force of law, because it is only a resolution by the general assembly. A resolution is only a recommendation to the states and is not legally binding.

But international law is based not just on treaty but also on custom. Over the years the Universal Declaration of Human Rights has come to reflect the general practice of the overwhelming majority of states. Moreover, most states feel an obligation to fulfill the norms of the Declaration. Therefore it is generally agreed that the Universal Declaration has attained the status of customary international law and in that sense is binding upon the states. The Declaration on the Elimination of All Forms of Intolerance and of Discrimination Based on Religion or Belief, like other declarations, has some legal effects and may eventually be considered as stating rules of customary international law. As Special Rapporteur Odio Benito pointed out, such declarations entail concrete "obligations of conduct, containing unquestionable values" that should govern the daily conduct of individuals and states.[10]

Since the 1981 Declaration addresses the development of international norms, brought to fruition through a long and delicate process, there are those who would argue that its status is "near-law". Very few states would openly say that they are not bound by it either legally or morally. Perhaps the best evidence of this is that governments feel obliged to respond to the communications from the Special Rapporteur who was appointed by the Commission in 1986, after it received reports of incidents and governmental actions inconsistent with the Declaration. Angelo Vidal d'Almeida Ribeiro of Portugal was mandated to examine these incidents and actions and to recommend remedial measures. (It is the annual reports of this Special Rapporteur which we looked at in detail in chapter 2.)

In the discussion in the UN Commission on Human Rights on the implementation of the Declaration, the director of the WCC's Commission of the Churches on International Affairs (CCIA) emphasized the need for the Commission to adopt an approach of dialogue between religious communities and their governments as well as among religious communities themselves. He asked the Commission (a) to inquire into and analyze the causes that might lead to or exacerbate discrimination or intolerance based on religion or belief; (b) to examine and keep under review the relevance of national legislation in this respect;

and (c) to examine socio-political changes and factors which may affect relationships among religious or belief communities and between them and their governments.[11]

Besides the Special Rapporteur, whose mandate has been extended from year to year, the other regular mechanism within the United Nations system for monitoring religious liberty is the Human Rights Committee under the International Covenant on Civil and Political Rights. Theo van Boven says:

> The two mechanisms have in common that both relate to the accountability of governments. However, the Human Rights Committee operates on the firm legal basis of a treaty, while the Special Rapporteur uses the Declaration as the yardstick. The Human Rights Committee exercises regular supervision on a periodic basis and takes primarily into account official materials provided by governments of states parties. But the Special Rapporteur is served with information relating to alleged violations and incidents and originating from a variety of sources, including those of the non-governmental sector. The Human Rights Committee deals with freedom of religion or belief together with the other human rights and fundamental freedoms enshrined in the Covenant. On the other hand, the Special Rapporteur's mandate is largely concentrated on alleged violations of religious rights and freedoms and aspects immediately related thereto.[12]

These two mechanisms are complementary and mutually reinforcing tools.

After itemizing some of the different ways in which religious intolerance continues to be manifested — ranging from denial of access to education, health services, passports and jobs to confiscation of property to physical assault and corporal punishment and, in the case of one country, capital punishment for "apostasy" — the Special Rapporteur in his 1991 report immediately linked these phenomena to the "enjoyment of human rights in general", including "fundamental rights and freedoms as the right to life, to liberty and security of the person, to physical integrity, the right to freedom of movement, the right to freedom of opinion and expression and the right to take part in public life".[13] Religious liberty, in other words, can be protected only along with other human rights. When other human rights are violated, religious liberty is curtailed and even transgressed — and vice versa.

The Special Rapporteur in his 1992 report again asked the states to consider the usefulness of preparing a binding international instrument. But he underlined the need for effective implementation of all relevant international human rights instruments.[14]

We may conclude our description of the evolution of international instruments related to religious liberty in this chapter with a brief reference to two related issues: the rights of religious minorities and the right to conscientious objection.

In view of the increasingly visible pluralism in many nations and the rising demands for group rights, it is not surprising that there is renewed discussion on minorities within the United Nations system. A draft declaration on minorities is before the Commission on Human Rights. International human rights law actually began as an attempt to protect groups discriminated against, particularly religious minorities. Already in the seventeenth century, several treaties incorporated clauses ensuring certain rights to individuals or groups whose religion differed from that of the majority. In some European and Middle Eastern countries domestic law incorporated provisions in favour of religious minorities.

The minority protection system of the League of Nations was a significant innovation, even though it eventually collapsed under the weight of the same developments which made the League itself collapse. The system was intended to ensure that nationals belonging to racial, religious or linguistic minorities would be placed in every respect on a footing of perfect equality with other nationals of the state. The minority provisions had the status of fundamental law in the respective states. The League of Nations had a special mechanism, the Minorities Section, to deal with the states under minority obligations.

As Lerner explains, after the second world war and with the founding of the United Nations, "emphasis in the protection of human rights shifted from 'group' protection to the protection of individual rights and freedoms, almost exclusively. The new approach was that whenever someone's rights were violated or restricted because of a group characteristic — race, religion, ethnic or national origin or culture — the matter could be taken care of by protecting the rights of the individual, on a purely individual basis, mainly by the principle of non-discrimination."[15] Whether this approach is satisfactory is now widely debated.

During the discussions on the draft of the Universal Declaration of Human Rights, proposals to include a provision on national minorities were rejected. The International Covenant on Civil and Political Rights, adopted in 1966, contains what is currently the only provision in international law on the rights of minorities. Article 27 reads: "In those states in which ethnic, religious or linguistic minorities exist, persons belonging to such minorities shall not be denied the right, in community with other members of their group, to enjoy their own culture, to profess and practise their own religion, or to use their own language." Whether this actually confers rights to members of a minority *as a group* has been much debated. It can be argued that the rights are given to "persons" only.

In 1990, the Special Rapporteur for the implementation of the Declaration on the Elimination of All Forms of Intolerance and of Discrimination Based on Religion or Belief sent a questionnaire to member states of the United Nations which included the following question: "How does your country protect the right of its citizens to practise their faith when they constitute a religious minority?"

Most of the responding governments said the right of all persons to practise their faith, whether they belong to a religious minority or whether they are citizens, residents or non-residents is protected by the law.[16] Some of the replies merit special mention. The Iranian government indicated that "minorities are protected by the government... in accordance with principles of the constitution and the law relating to the affairs of personal status of non-Shi'a Iranians". The Syrian government stated that the Jewish and Christian minority communities benefitted from the necessary *de jure* and *de facto* protection. The government of Morocco stated that there is "very high toleration in Morocco for the religions of the Book". The government of Indonesia indicated that it did "not adopt the terms majority and minority as these words are generally understood", adding that its citizens were "first and foremost Indonesians, with the inherent right to adhere to the religion of (their) choice".[17]

On the basis of specific incidents of religious intolerance brought to his attention, however, the Special Rapporteur observed in his 1992 report "that minority religious groups are often not able to practise their religion freely in many countries". Problems especially arise in countries with one official religion, but even in countries whose constitution recognizes and provides guarantees for a number of religions, the freedom to practise them may not always be equal. And even where there is no official recognized religion, the freedom to practise may be greater for some religions than others.[18]

The question of the right to refuse to take part in military service has been before the United Nations almost from its very beginning. In fact, as Martin MacPherson points out, the issue already arose in the League of Nations, which in the late 1920s turned down a proposal from the Soviet Union "to abolish all forms of military service, including military education of youth by the state or public societies".

In 1972, the International Commission of Jurists published a study summarizing laws on conscientious objection in 150 countries. The 1984 Commission on Human Rights received a report and recommendations on the subject. In the same year there was an appeal to the Commission initiated by the Friends World Committee for Consultation and endorsed by the WCC and several other non-governmental organizations, to accept the recommendations. Three years later the Commission passed a resolution supporting recognition of conscientious objection to military service "as a legitimate exercise of the right to freedom of thought, conscience and religion".

The Special Rapporteur's 1992 report includes a summary of responses to a questionnaire which asked governments: "How does your country deal with conscientious objection to compulsory military service?" In general, of course, this issue arises only in countries where military service is mandatory. In many of the countries where conscientious objection is permitted, mainly Western European countries, armed service in the military may be replaced by alternative service in non-combat units or by civilian service.[19]

Among countries which do not permit conscientious objection to military service, the relevant laws are not applied with the same severity. Exemptions are usually made with regard to persons belonging to or training for certain religious professions or persons whose faith does not allow them to bear arms.

The position of Switzerland merits special mention. The report said that although a conscript may not be exempted from military service on the basis of his religious beliefs, the government indicated that persons "who would experience a serious conflict of conscience by the use of a weapon because of their religious or moral beliefs may perform service without weapons". Nevertheless, conscientious objection continues to be an offence.[20]

The governments of a number of countries where conscientious objection to military service is not admitted maintain that the performance of military service was an honour for all citizens and a sacred obligation.

In conclusion, governments today generally seem to consider themselves more accountable to the international community on matters of religious liberty than in the past. This is evident from the fact that they feel obliged to take the enquiries from the UN seriously. Nevertheless, we have also seen that infringements of religious liberty continue to take place in many parts of the world, sometimes involving serious isolations of the rights of individuals and groups. Efforts to strengthen UN mechanisms and procedures, as well as consistent use of existing mechanisms and instruments, deserve support from churches and from all who are concerned about religious liberty.

NOTES

[1] Quoted by Theo van Boven, "Religious Liberty in the Context of Human Rights", in *The Ecumenical Review*, vol. 37, no. 3, 1985, p.348.
[2] *Ibid.*
[3] Natan Lerner, *Group Rights and Discrimination in International Law*, Dordrecht, Netherlands, Martinus Nijhoff, 1991, p.77.
[4] *Ibid*, p.78.
[5] Theo van Boven "Advances and Obstacles in Building Understanding and Respect Between Peoples of Diverse Religions and Belief", *Human Rights Quarterly*, vol. 13, no. 4, November 1991, p.439.
[6] B.R. Ramcharan, "Towards a Universal Standard of Religious Liberty", *Religious Liberty: CCIA Background Information*, 1987, no.1, p.9.
[7] Elizabeth Odio Benito, *Study on the Current Dimensions of the Problems of Intolerance and Discrimination on Grounds of Religion or Belief*, United Nations, Commission on Human Rights, 1986, p.4.
[8] *Ibid*, p.52.

[9] Theo van Boven, Working Paper for the United Nations on Elimination of All Forms of Intolerance and of Discrimination Based on Religion or Belief, Geneva, UN Centre for Human Rights, 1989.
[10] Benito, *op cit.*, p.49.
[11] *The Churches in International Affairs, Reports 1983-86*, Geneva, WCC, 1987, p.67.
[12] Theo van Boven, "Advances and Obstacles", *op. cit.*, p.436.
[13] Report submitted by Angelo Vidal d'Almeida Ribeiro on the Implementation of the Declaration on the Elimination of All Forms of Intolerance and of Discrimination Based on Religion or Belief, Geneva, United Nations, Commission on Human Rights, 1991, p.119.
[14] Report to the Forty-Eighth Session of the Commission on Human Rights, Geneva, United Nations, 1991.
[15] Lerner, *op. cit*, p.14.
[16] Report of the Special Rapporteur, Geneva, United Nations, 1992, p.161.
[17] *Ibid.*
[18] *Ibid.*, p.162.
[19] Report of the Special Rapporteur, 1992, *op. cit.*, pp.164-166.
[20] *Ibid*, p.119.

10. Conclusion

The declaration by the first assembly of the WCC nearly half a century ago that "an essential element in a good international order is freedom of religion" has lost none of its validity. Indeed, amidst contemporary discussions of a "new world order", the close relationship between religious liberty and peace is more evident than ever before, because of the increasingly important role played by religion in national and international affairs. Peace depends on human freedoms, and religious liberty is perhaps the most precious of such freedoms.

Religious pluralism, which is now a worldwide phenomenon, demands a greater understanding of the religion of the other — an understanding that must lead to greater respect and dialogue. There was a time when a person speaking of religion could refer only to his or her own faith, like Parson Thwackum in Henry Fielding's novel *Tom Jones*: "When I mention religion, I mean the Christian religion, and not only the Christian religion, but the Protestant religion, and not only the Protestant religion but the Church of England."

That is no longer the case. Today when we "mention religion", we must mean all religions. And when we speak of religious liberty, we have to speak of religious liberty for all. In a pluralistic world, each religious faith has to affirm equal freedom for all other faiths, irrespective of their beliefs. The "Williamsburg Charter" states this clearly: "A right for a Protestant is a right for an Orthodox is a right for a Catholic is a right for a humanist is a right for a Mormon is a right for a Muslim is a right for a Buddhist — and the followers of any other faith."

We have seen the importance of moving beyond mere religious toleration — a kind of grudging allowance of the existence of religious beliefs and practices other than one's own. Tolerance alone only creates different categories of citizens within a country; and that falls short of what pluralism requires — full religious liberty for all, with adherents of every religion and belief treating adherents of every other with full respect as equal fellow human beings.

Pluralism was once described by W.A. Visser 't Hooft, the first general secretary of the WCC, as a situation "in which various religious, philosophical and ideological concepts live side by side and in which none of them holds a privileged status".[1] The resurgence of national cultures and nationalisms with strong religious content, the presence of large immigrant communities with a different religion, as well as the renewed emphasis on such human rights as liberty of conscience have all sharpened the profile of religious pluralism. Especially in the West, churches which have been accustomed to living in mono-cultural and even mono-religious situations are now finding themselves in multi-religious contexts. This has compelled them to rethink many of their assumptions about other religions and their relationship to them. Within the ecumenical movement, they have begun to take seriously the experiences of churches in the Middle East and Asia who have lived for centuries side by side with people of other living faiths.

This is a good beginning. The new consciousness of the presence and relevance of other religions requires casting away stereotypes of one another and replacing them with authentic pictures. A high degree of sensitivity to other religions, reinforced by respect for them, is essential.

In the face of the tensions between religious groups in many countries, the volatility of the mixture of religion and politics and the violence generated or fuelled in the name of religion, we should not ignore the fact that many religious communities of the world have expressed a growing awareness of and commitment to what it means to be global. A statement made by the World Conference on Religion and Peace in Kyoto, Japan, in 1970, lists some of these emerging understandings: "a conviction of the fundamental unity of the human family..., a sense of the sacredness of each individual person and his conscience, a sense of the value of the human community..., a realization that might is not right, that human power is not self-sufficient and absolute..., a sense of obligation to stand on the side of the poor and oppressed as against the rich and the oppressors and a profound hope that good will finally prevail".[2]

The churches and others concerned for religious liberty can undertake a number of tasks to promote it:

- Full use of communication and educational channels to raise awareness about the importance of religious liberty as a fundamental human right which is especially essential for peace in the world.

- Systematic efforts to understand and appreciate other religions, actively promoting not just toleration but full liberty and respect for them.
- Historical research into the role played by violations of religious liberty in the decline and destruction of societies.
- Close monitoring of the status of religious liberty in one's own country, identifying the causes of violations and intolerance that exist and undertaking remedial actions, if necessary with international support and solidarity.
- Full use of the mechanism and instruments of the United Nations system, underlining the international accountability of governments regarding religious liberty and other human rights, as well as support for efforts to strengthen UN mechanisms and procedures in this area.
- Promotion of inter-religious dialogue, in the recognition that religious communities, as well as states, can be violators of religious liberty.

Full religious liberty includes not only freedom from outside coercion and suppression but also from the suppression or restriction of human rights within each particular religious or belief community. As Robert Gordis points out: "The first and oldest aspect of religious liberty is the right which a group claims for itself to practise its faith without interference from others... Only later and half-heartedly is freedom of conscience extended to other groups who differ in belief and practice." But it is only even later — after a much longer struggle (which has scarcely begun in most religious communities) — that the highest stage of religious liberty emerges, "when a religious group, dedicated to its belief and tradition, is willing to grant freedom of thought and action to dissidents within its own ranks".[3]

An essential element of genuine pluralism is inter-religious dialogue. For the past couple of decades, the WCC has played an active role in promoting this, not emphasizing "dialogue as an end in itself, but as one of the ways through which people could seek community in pluralistic situations".[4]

At a WCC consultation in 1977 in Chiang Mai, Thailand, participants identified two levels of dialogue: one involving the growing majority of Christians who live "in actual community with people who may be committed to faiths and ideologies other than our own", the other rooted in an awareness of "concerns beyond the local", which leads to "a dialogue between communities, in which we tackle issues of national and international concern, for the sake of the vision of a worldwide 'community of communities'".[5]

The consultation recognized dialogue as a way in which Christians can be more obedient to the commandment not to "bear false witness" against their neighbours. Dialogue helps to prevent us from disfiguring the image of our neighbours of different faiths. It presupposes mutual trust and respect for the integrity of each participant.

Significant progress in dialogue has been made at the international level with sponsoring and initiatives from the WCC, the Vatican and other groups, usually from the side of the churches. However, there are fewer examples of advances in dialogue at the national level, where the problems of interfaith relations are often most acute. In many places, religious groups have yet to talk among themselves seriously at this level. Like ecumenism, dialogue at the international level is often easier than at home.

This book is being published during the year that marks the 500th anniversary of the expulsion of the Jews from Spain. King Ferdinand and Queen Isabella's campaign to "purify" Roman Catholic Spain culminated in 1492, first with the defeat of Granada, Islam's last stronghold in Christian Europe, then with the royal degree banning Judaism. As Howard LaFranchi has written, "the Jewish expulsion alone does not capture the full significance of what Spain lost, nor does the end of Islam's rule over its last piece of the Iberian peninsula... What gives these events particular importance is that they mark the end of a unique era that brought together in Spain the three great monotheistic religions born and developed in the crucible of the Mediterranean basin." The radical aspect of 1492 was to abolish a unique historical moment of coexistence and dialogue among the three "religions of the Book". It was in Spain — where it could and should have been born — that the possibility of an open and tolerant Europe was in fact destroyed.[6]

It is important to recall this event in history which by destroying religious coexistence set back the course of human progress. It is also important to recall periods in history when genuine pluralism not only ensured full religious liberty for all but accelerated the course of civilization. We need to take seriously lessons from past events and insights from earlier periods. Promoting religious harmony is one important way to contribute to peace. Today, one major threat to peace comes from violations of religious liberty and intolerance on the basis of religion and belief. Hence the urgency of giving more attention to religious liberty.

Fundamental to humanity is an inescapable quest for meaning and belonging, for making sense of life and finding community. This urge to find meaning is as precious as life itself. It finds expression in ultimate beliefs. Religious liberty is the freedom to uphold such beliefs free from any coercion. Its basis is the God-given and inviolable dignity of the human being. It is intertwined with freedom of conscience. The right to religious liberty in its essence is inalienable and non-negotiable. The affirmation of religious liberty is inseparable from Christian witness. The defence of religious liberty is thus integral to the mission of the church.

NOTES

[1] W.A. Visser 't Hooft, "Pluralism — Temptation and Opportunity", *The Ecumenical Review*, vol. XVIII, no. 2, April 1966, p.129.
[2] Cf. Homer A. Jack ed., *Religion for Peace*, New Delhi, Gandhi Peace Foundation, 1973, p.ix.
[3] Robert Gordis, quoted by Leonard Swidler in *Religious Liberty and Human Rights*, Philadelphia, Ecumenical Press, 1986, p.xv.
[4] Stanley Samartha, *Faith in the Midst of Faiths*, Geneva, WCC, 1977, p.12.
[5] *Ibid.*, p.143.
[6] Howard LaFranchi, "The End of Tolerance", *Christian Science Monitor*, 1 April 1992.